Beyond

Knitting Adventures With
Judy's Magic Cast-On

Judy Becker

Photography by
Vivian Aubrey

Copyright © 2010 Judy A Becker

Photographs pages 9 and 10, and page 11 upper right: from the collection of the author
Photograph page 11 lower right, © 2005 Judy A Becker

All other photography © 2011 Vivian Aubrey

All rights reserved. The written instructions, photographs, designs, projects, and patterns in this volume are intended for the personal, non-commercial use of the reader and may be reproduced only for that purpose, and for inclusion of brief passages in an article or review. Any other use, including commercial use, is forbidden without written permission of the copyright holder.

Published by
Indigo Frog Press, PO Box 2054, Beaverton, Oregon 97075

First printed 2011
Printed and bound by Friesens in Manitoba, Canada

Publisher's Cataloging-In-Publication Data
(Prepared by The Donohue Group, Inc.)

Becker, Judy (Judy A.)
 Beyond toes : knitting adventures with Judy's Magic Cast-On / Judy Becker ; photography by Vivian Aubrey.

 p. : ill. ; cm.

 "Over The Top Mittens first published in Twists and Turns The Newsletter for Lovers of Cable Knitting, in the Winter 2009 issue."--T.p. verso.
  ISBN: 978-0-9844619-0-5

 1. Knitting--Patterns. 2. Knitting--Handbooks, manuals, etc. I. Aubrey, Vivian. II. Title.

TT820 .B43 2011
746.43/041   2011911386

To Adam

Who will wear his mom's hand knits
and brag about them to his friends.

Love you!

Beyond Toes

Contents

Treasure Map 6

How To Use This Book 7

Introduction 8

Techniques 12

Judy's Magic Cast-On—Port JMCO   14
Knitting From Both Directions—Provisional Bay 16
Invisible Cast-On for Ribbing—Tubular Reef   17
Twisted I-Cord Circular Cast-On—I-Cord Island 18
Adding Stitches With JMCO—Magic Bridge   20
Double Knitting With JMCO—Double Straits   22

Hats 23

Laurel Jane's Cap   24
Haberdasher   30
Charlie's Creature Cap   40
Headbumps   44
Leaves A Fall'n   48

Neckwear 53

Magic Cowl & Wristlet   54
Eye Of The Needle   62
Monica's Seamen's Scarf   68
Swept Off My Feet   74

Mittens 79

Bobsled Mittens   80
Over The Top Mittens   86

Socks 91

Spring Fever Socks   92
Three-Point Socks   98

Garments & Wraps 105

Djinn   106
Pasarela   114
November Street   120
Mokosh   126
Poncho Puzzle   136

Bags & Cozies 141

Blockalicious   142
Cabled Netbook Cozy   148
FlatPack   156

Comfy Things 161

Branches & Round-Up   162
Pippa   166

References 171

Abbreviations & Symbols   172
About The Designers   176
Resources   180
Acknowledgements   182
Endnotes   183
Photo credits   183
Index of Patterns By Technique   184

Beyond Toes

Treasure Map

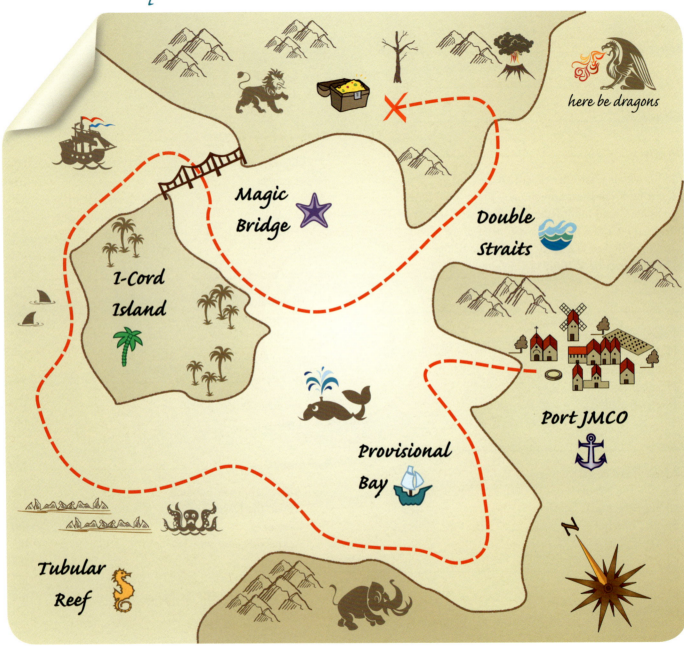

Beyond Toes

How To Use This Book

Judy's Magic Cast-On (JMCO) is the port from which we will launch all of our knitting adventures.

The treasure map on the previous page shows one path that you might take on this journey. But you may explore in any direction and any order you wish.

If you are not already familiar with Judy's Magic Cast-On, start by learning the standard JMCO—Port JMCO. From there, you can follow the path to the treasure by learning each of the other techniques in the order they are shown, or you can forge your own path by learning the techniques needed for projects in the order you want to knit them.

On the very last page of the book, all of the projects are listed according to the JMCO technique that is used.

Be sure to note the icons on the map. There is a different symbol for each technique. The icons can be found on the instruction pages for each technique and on the pages of the patterns that use it. This anchor symbol, for example, can be found on page 14 and page 15, along with the instructions for the standard Judy's Magic Cast-On method. It can also be found right below the page number on the pages of the patterns that use the standard JMCO.

The projects do not have assigned difficulty levels because terms like "easy" and "hard" mean different things to different knitters. Read the pattern carefully to make your own assessment. But don't be afraid to jump in! This is an adventure after all.

The techniques included here are not the only ways to use JMCO. Can you find new methods by exploring "off the map?"

Introduction

𝒦nitting has been an adventure for me.

My maternal grandmother, Estella Cunningham Lechleiter, was born into a large family at the end of the Victorian era. Like all ladies of that time, Grandma and her sisters—known collectively by everyone in town as The Aunts—were accomplished at handicrafts of all kinds. They made many lovely things, some of which grace my house even now.

The Cunningham family, and my paternal forebears the Fannings, moved to southeastern Idaho in the early 1900s. The west was in many places still a wild and somewhat unsettled territory, and the pioneering spirit was apparent.

I grew up surrounded by strong, accomplished women and men who believed that adventure was not only fun, but a necessary part of life. From Mama and Dads I learned to love the woods and the mountains, to find adventure everywhere I went, and to find humor in the odd and sometimes not very fun things that might happen along the way.

"We will laugh at this later," Mama would say as the bear ate all of our food, or the wind blew the tent down, or the fish escaped. And, although we disagreed with her mightily at the time, she was right; eventually we would laugh.

Mama was not drawn to the crafts that Grandma and The Aunts practiced. "I'm not good with my hands," she would explain. Hers were hands that could whip up a meal over a campfire, plant a garden, and bandage a skinned knee, but not hem a pair of pants.

So it was that armed with a book at age 8 or 9, I taught myself to crochet. After an offhand remark from one of The Aunts that I might enjoy making doilies, I became an obsessive wielder of tiny hooks and thread.

A few years later I joined a 4-H Club. Because we were all "town kids" without the facilities to raise farm animals, we learned cooking, sewing and knitting. Our knitting instructor was a lovely and patient woman who owned a local yarn shop and did not at all mind a gaggle of giggly girls armed with pointy sticks invading her territory.

I know I knit a number of projects because I still have my old needles and they are of various sizes. But the two objects I remember best were a horrible white sweater and a brown poncho.

The sweater was knit from a scratchy white wool. The front was shorter than the back because I got tired of knitting it. Blocking did not help, and so I learned that gauge is an important thing after all. I wore it once, under protest, because Mama insisted.

"The Aunts" visiting Yellowstone—Lake Lodge, July, 1925

Road Trip near Mackay, ID

Introduction ⚜ Beyond Toes

Lechleiter family: Grandpa, Grandma, Aunt Georgianne (on trike), Alice (Mama)

John & Alice Fanning

The poncho was knit from acrylic faux "mohair" and was acres of brown stockinette with white Fair Isle snowflakes around the hem. I loved it dearly and wore it until it fell apart.

But knitting seemed so slow to me, after crochet. Other than occasionally replacing the slippers that Mama loved, I set aside my knitting needles, and for many years pursued a variety of other crafts. I was always making something, but knitting held little allure.

I managed to keep the spirit of adventure alive in my life, at least every now and then. I have never been one who reveled in the adrenalin rush of roller coasters, sky diving, or like pursuits. But my son, Adam, and I would take road trips in the summer. Rather than planning ahead (much), Adam would spin a game spinner, and in whichever direction the arrow pointed we would head out on our little expeditions. I would drive until we saw something that caught our fancy, then we would stop for the night, see the local sights, and head out again the next morning. We had a lot of fun exploring.

And then Adam, got a learner's permit.

Anyone who has taught a teenager to drive will tell you that it can be a nerve-wracking experience. I found myself in need of something to keep my hands busy so that I refrained from grabbing the steering wheel or throwing open the door to bail out. (That last may be a slight exaggeration.)

The thought came unbidden to my mind: I'll just knit a pair of socks.

Somewhere along the way I had learned how to use double-pointed needles. I had never knit a sock, but it sounded adventurous and I was willing to give it a try.

I picked up DPNs and yarn and stared at them in my hands. I couldn't remember even how to cast on.

Thank goodness for the marvel that is the internet. I searched for sock knitting techniques and was surprised to learn that many people knit socks from the top down. Perhaps because I can be contrary and a wee bit stubborn, starting at the toe made more sense to me. I found instructions for a toe-up sock and I began knitting while Adam began driving. Although I often ended up fumbling to pick up dropped stitches in a moving car at night, I was instantly hooked and knitting was back in my life.

That first pair of toe-up socks has been followed by many socks, bags, sweaters, scarves, hats and mittens.

The only cloud over my otherwise sunny new love of knitting was the cast-on for a toe-up sock. I tried every one that I could find mention of. While they all worked fine, none were perfect for me. So I began the search for a better way.

One day I was sick. I had been very ill with the flu, but I was recovering. I had reached the stage where I could no longer stand to stay in bed, but I didn't feel good enough to do anything productive like reading or knitting. I sat in my rocking chair, a cup of tea close to hand, and decided that now might be a good time to look for that better cast on.

I gathered all of my knitting reference books and began methodically going through them looking for something I could use or modify. Nothing worked. Eventually I just began winding yarn around a pair of needles barely paying attention to what I was doing.

All of a sudden I had a beautiful, invisible cast-on, with no idea how I'd gotten there. But, having done so once, I knew I could again. I started over, this time paying closer attention.

Once recovered from my illness, and now able to recreate the cast-on nine times out of ten, I showed it to a group of knitters at Tangle Knitting Studio, a local yarn shop now sadly lost to the community. I was surprised by the enthusiasm with which my little trick was embraced. The consensus was that other knitters would be interested, and I should find a way to spread the word. I offered the instructions to the online magazine Knitty.com, and Judy's Magic Cast-On (JMCO) was published in the Spring, 2006 issue.

Although originally meant as a cast-on for toe-up socks, JMCO can be used almost any place an invisible cast-on is needed. It makes a stable provisional cast-on, and it can be used to simplify some complicated techniques such as the tubular cast-on. As I play with JMCO, I find more and more ways that I can use it.

This book includes instruction for the basic Judy's Magic Cast-On, plus several other techniques that use JMCO as a base. Twenty-one adventurous designers have contributed patterns to showcase each of the methods.

I hope that you will try these ideas and explore other ways to incorporate JMCO into your knitting.

Ready? Let's go!

Close encounter with a frog. Judy & John (Dads)

Adam in Death Valley

A Few Tips To Get You Started

- Judy's Magic Cast-On, like anything new, may seem awkward at first. But once you get into its rhythm, it's fun and easy to do.

- The instructions that follow are written for two circular needles. You can easily modify the instructions to use one long circular needle (magic loop) or a set of double-point needles (DPNs).

- It can be easy to cast on too tightly. If you find the first row hard to knit, you might try casting on using needles one size larger than specified by the pattern.

- You might find it helpful at first to use a multi-colored yarn or to tie two colors of yarn together so it is clear which is the working yarn and which is the tail. You can also use two needles that are different colors or one that is wood and one that is metal.

- The illustrations are colored to make the instructions easier to follow. The yarn tail is yellow and the working yarn (the yarn strand going to the ball) is blue. One needle is light tan and the other needle is darker brown.

- If you are familiar with the long-tail cast-on, you will find that the yarn is held in a very similar manner. But it's not exactly the same. Be careful to hold the tail over the index finger and the working yarn over the thumb. This is the opposite of the long tail cast-on.

- Be careful to keep the top needle always on the top, and the bottom needle always on the bottom. Don't flip the needles or turn them over.

- Some knitters find it easier to move their left hand to wrap the yarn around the needles. Some find it easier to swing the needles back and forth like a pendulum, moving the needles to the yarn, while keeping their left hand still. And still other knitters use a combination of hand and needle movement. Try them all to see what works best for you.

- The yarn can be wrapped in either direction around the needles without changing the result. The "magic" happens between the needles as knit stitches are formed.

- The illustrations show the yarn wrapped counter-clockwise, which will result in stitches that are mounted with their leading legs in front of the needle.

- Wrapping the yarn clockwise will result in stitches that are mounted with their leading legs behind the needle.

- Be sure to knit all stitches through their leading legs on the first round to prevent twisted stitches.

- Because you actually create the first row of knitting as you cast on, JMCO is invisible from both sides. It can be used in places where it's not desirable to see a cast-on edge or the ridge caused by picking up stitches.

- JMCO is a very stable cast-on. You can easily cast on any number of stitches—hundreds if you want—without worrying that the cast-on will fall apart. In fact, after casting on you can carefully remove one of the needles and the cast on loops will remain. (If you take out both needles, though, it will fall apart.)

Techniques Beyond Toes

Judy's Magic Cast-On — Port JMCO

Judy's Magic Cast-On is the basis for the techniques on the following pages. See page 13 for a few tips and tricks to help you get started. Once you've learned JMCO, refer to the Treasure Map on page 184 to see which patterns use each technique.

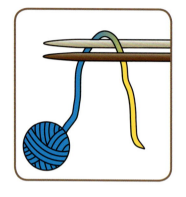  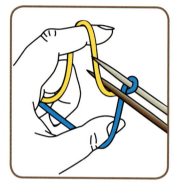 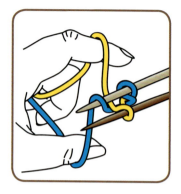

1 Hold the needles with the tips pointing to your left and the light tan needle above the dark brown needle. Pull a long tail of yarn from your ball and lay the yarn across the light tan top needle with the blue working yarn hanging behind the light tan top needle and the yellow tail hanging in front. Bring the dark brown bottom needle below the light tan top needle and in front of the yellow tail yarn.

2 Hold the yarn in your left hand with the yellow tail yarn over your index finger and the blue working yarn under your thumb. Your other fingers hold the strands and apply tension. Be careful not to apply too much tension! The yarn should run freely through your fingers or the cast on will be too tight.

The loop made around the light tan top needle is the first cast on stitch. You might find it helpful to hold this stitch in place with a finger of your right hand.

3 Bring the yellow tail yarn under the dark brown bottom needle, around it to the front, and then back between the two needles making a loop around the dark brown bottom needle. As you maneuver the yarn and needles, be careful to keep the same side of the needles facing you and the dark brown needle always below the light tan top needle.

Now two stitches are cast on: the original blue loop around the light tan top needle and the new yellow loop around the dark brown bottom needle.

4 Bring the blue working yarn to the front between the two needles, then over the light tan top needle, making a loop around the light tan top needle.

You now have three stitches cast on: two blue stitches on the light tan top needle and one yellow stitch on the dark brown bottom needle.

Judy's Magic Cast-On — Port JMCO

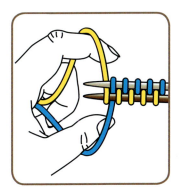 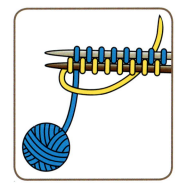  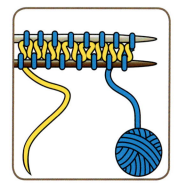

5 Repeat steps 3 and 4 until you have cast on the number of stitches needed for your project. Be careful not to pull the loops too tightly around the needles. End with step 3. Because the first stitch cast on was with the blue working yarn, casting on the last stitch with the yellow tail yarn ensures that the same number of stitches are on each needle.

If you turn your needles over and look at the back, you will see a row of purl bumps. JMCO creates the first row of knitting as you cast on.

6 Bring the yellow tail yarn to the front below both needles, around the blue working yarn. Hold the tail against the needles as you begin knitting to secure the last stitch cast on. Once you have knit the first stitch, you don't need to hold the tail any more.

You have completed the cast-on.

If the pattern specifies knitting in the round, the next two illustrations show how to knit the first round. If your pattern specifies knitting flat, continue to page 16 for those instructions.

7 Rotate the needles clockwise so the tips are pointing to your right. The yellow tail yarn on the dark brown needle is now on top, and the blue working yarn on the light tan needle is on the bottom. Unless the pattern specifies otherwise, be sure that the smooth side of the loops is facing you and the purl bumps are not facing you.

Pull the light tan needle to the right until the blue stitches are on the cable. Knit the yellow stitches using the free end of the dark brown needle. In the pattern instructions, the dark brown needle will be referred to as needle #1.

8 The yellow tail yarn has formed the row of stitches between the two needles. Rotate the needles clockwise again.

Pull the dark brown needle to the right until the stitches are on the cable. Push the light tan needle to the left until the stitches are on it, ready to knit.

Knit the stitches from the light tan needle using its free end. In the pattern instructions, the light tan needle will be referred to as needle #2.

You have knit the first round. Continue working according to the pattern instructions.

Techniques ⚓ *Beyond Toes*

Knitting From Both Directions — Provisional Bay

A provisional cast-on is one that enables knitting in two directions. Judy's Magic Cast-On works very well as a provisional cast-on because it is stable and invisible, and does not require waste yarn.

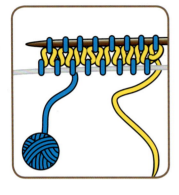 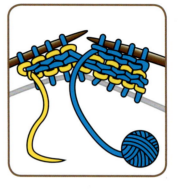 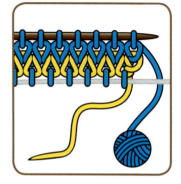

1 Following steps 1 to 6 of JMCO (see page 14), cast on the number of stitches required for your pattern.

At the end of step 6, work the first row of the pattern as follows:
If the pattern specifies stockinette stitch, turn the needles so the smooth side is facing you and work across the dark brown needle.
If the pattern specifies garter stitch, turn the needles so the purl bump side is facing you and work across the light tan needle.

The illustrations on this page show stockinette stitch.

2 At the end of the first row, do not rotate the needles clockwise. You will work only on one needle. The stitches on the other needle will rest on the cable until the pattern instructs you to start knitting the other direction.

If the pattern specifies flat knitting, turn the needles so that the purl bump side is facing you.

If the pattern specifies knitting in the round, do not turn; join to begin working in the round.

3 Using the free end of the needle, work the second row or round of your pattern across the stitches on that needle.

If the pattern specifies flat knitting, turn back to the knit side again at the end of the second row.

4 Continue working the first side according to your pattern instructions.

The resting stitches can stay on the cable so they are ready to work when your pattern specifies. Or, you can move the resting stitches to a stitch holder or waste yarn if you prefer.

Beyond Toes ~ Techniques

Invisible Cast-On for Ribbing — Tubular Reef

A tubular cast-on provides a stretchy and nearly invisible edge for ribbing. It's sometimes helpful to cast on and work the first round using needles one size larger than called for by your pattern. You will need a 3rd needle in the pattern size.

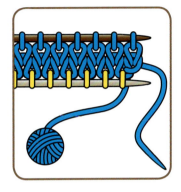 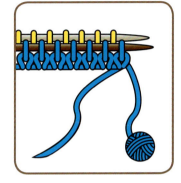  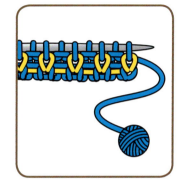

1 Complete all eight steps of Judy's Magic Cast-On (see page 14). For k1p1 ribbing, continue with instructions below. For k2p2 ribbing, work a second round and then continue.

In these illustrations, the yellow stitches will be purled in subsequent steps and the blue stitches will be knit.

2 Hold the needles in your left hand, parallel to the floor with the points to the right. The dark brown needle will be closer to you and the light tan needle will be further away.

The purl bump side should be up and the smooth side down.

Fold the work so that the needles are together and the knitting is below the needles.

3 Use a 3rd needle in the size specified by your pattern. Knit the first stitch from the dark brown needle. For k2p2 ribbing, knit the first two stitches from the dark brown needle.

Then purl the first stitch from the light tan needle. For K2P2 ribbing, purl the first two stitches from the light tan needle.

Repeat knitting 1 (or 2) stitches from the dark brown needle, followed by purling 1 (or 2) stitches from the light tan needle, until all stitches have been worked.

4 All of the stitches are now on a single needle.

Continue ribbing according to your pattern instructions.

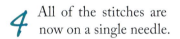

Techniques — Beyond Toes

Twisted I-Cord Circular Cast-On — I-Cord Island

When Deb Barnhill first showed the I-cord JMCO to me, I knew that it had to be included in this book! It makes a cute start for a baby cap or any project that starts with a small circle and could benefit from a "handle" in the center.

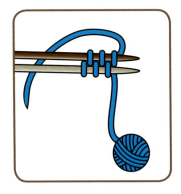 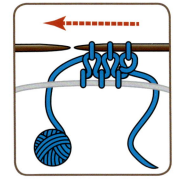 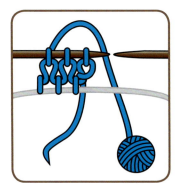 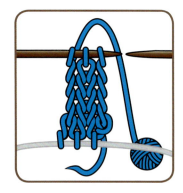

1 Following steps 1 to 6 of JMCO (see page 14), cast on the number of stitches called for by your pattern. This will be a small number of stitches—typically 3 or 4 stitches on each needle.

2 Knit across the stitches on the dark brown needle using the free end of the dark brown needle.

Do not turn the needles after knitting the first row.

Slide the stitches back to the original dark brown needle.

3 Pull the working yarn snugly across the back of the stitches and knit another row.

4 Repeat steps 2 and 3 until the I-cord is the length specified by your pattern.

You will notice that the knitting forms a cord-like tube.

Twisted I-Cord Circular Cast-On — I-Cord Island

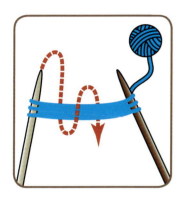
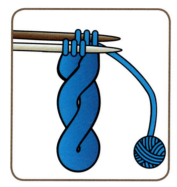
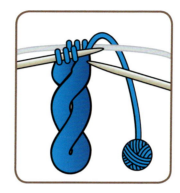

5 Hold the needles with the points up, with the I-cord stretched between them. The dark brown needle will be on the right and the light tan needle will be on the left.

Rotate the tip of the light tan needle behind the I-cord, underneath it, and then back around the front, twisting the I-cord.

Twist the I-cord the number of times specified by your pattern.

6 Hold the needles together, allowing the I-cord to twist around itself.

The light tan needle will be closer to you and the dark brown needle will be further away.

Make sure that the working yarn is coming from the stitch closest to the point of the dark brown needle. Be careful not to loop the working yarn over the needle, adding an extra stitch accidentally.

7 Pull the dark brown needle to the right so that the stitches are on the cable.

Using the free end of the light tan needle, knit the stitches from the light tan needle.

Rotate the needles so that the dark brown needle is closer to you and the light tan needle is further away.

8 Pull the light tan needle to the right so that the stitches are on the cable.

Push the dark brown needle to the left until the stitches are on the needle.

Using the free end of the dark brown needle, knit the stitches from the dark brown needle.

You have now knit one round. Continue with your pattern instructions.

Techniques ~ Beyond Toes

Adding Stitches With JMCO—Magic Bridge

This technique was developed by Jeny Staiman, who was kind enough to share it with me for this book. It is useful if, after you have worked for some ways, you need to cast on stitches and then knit the new stitches in both directions.

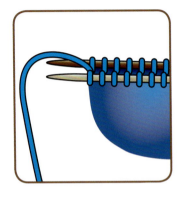 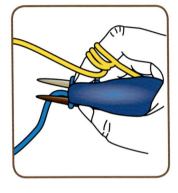 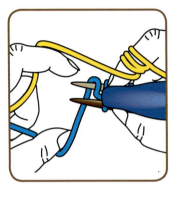 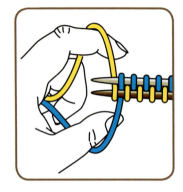

1 The stitches must be divided between two separate circular needles. If you have been working with the magic loop method, transfer half of the stitches to a second circular needle.

After completing the Magic Bridge cast-on, you will be knitting with the light tan needle. The stitches on the dark brown needle will rest.

2 You will need a second strand of working yarn. This can come from either a separate ball of yarn, or the other end of the ball you have been knitting with. In these illustrations, the original working yarn is blue, and the second strand of yarn is yellow.

Pull out a tail of yellow yarn that is long enough to complete the cast-on. Wrap the yarn around your finger a couple of times to anchor it and hold the yellow working yarn in your hand.

Hold the needles with the tips pointing to the left and the knitted fabric towards you.

3 Hold the long tail of the yellow yarn over your left forefinger with the yellow ball to your right.

Hold the blue working yarn under your thumb. Use your other fingers to secure the yarn.

Because there is no loop of yarn to create the first stitch, you will need to start JMCO with step 4 to add a stitch of blue yarn to the light tan needle (see page 14).

Then complete JMCO step 3 to add a yellow stitch to the dark brown needle.

4 Repeat JMCO steps 4 and 3 until you have cast on the number of stitches specified by your pattern.

You will need to secure the yellow tail while the yellow stitches rest. You can tie it in a loose half-hitch around the blue working yarn. Untie the knot when you weave the ends in.

If the pattern instructs you to join the new stitches to the existing knitting and begin knitting in the round, continue with steps 5 through 8. If the pattern specifies to work flat, follow step 3 of "Knitting From Both Directions—Provisional Bay" on page 16

Adding Stitches With JMCO—Magic Bridge

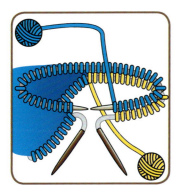 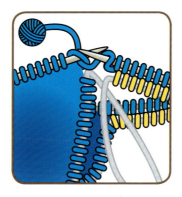 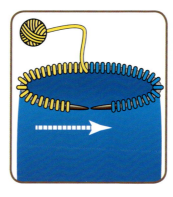 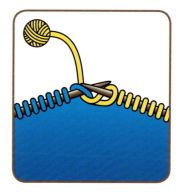

5 Being careful to keep the cables from twisting, bring the tips of the light brown needles together.

Depending on the number of stitches you have cast on, you may need to pull up a loop of cable on the opposite side of the work from the needle tips in order to use the magic loop technique.

6 Join the stitches on the light tan needle and begin working in the round.

The stitches on the dark brown needle—both the original blue stitches and the new yellow stitches—will rest for now.

7 When you have completed the first part of your knitting, or when your pattern specifies, turn the knitting over so that the dark brown needle is on top.

You may need to slide the stitches along the needle until you come to the first yellow stitch and the yellow working yarn.

8 Begin knitting with the yellow working yarn, knitting in the round or as specified by your pattern.

There may be a gap between the blue stitches and the yellow stitches on both sides of the yellow stitches. You can eliminate the gap by picking up an extra stitch between the blue and yellow stitches on each side. On the next round, decrease these extra stitches away by knitting each together with the blue stitch next to it.

Techniques ~ Beyond Toes

Double Knitting With JMCO — Double Straits

Double knitting creates a fabric that has two smooth knit sides on a double-walled construction. Because JMCO allows you to cast on with two different colors of yarn, it creates an invisible start for double knitting.

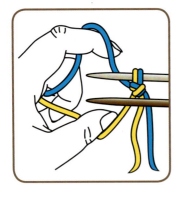 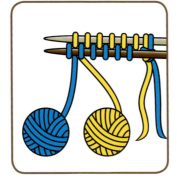 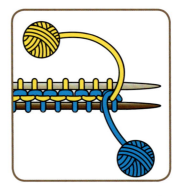 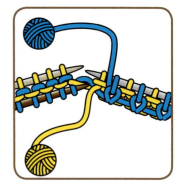

1 In these illustrations, the main color is blue and the contrasting color is yellow. Both strands represent working yarn.

You will need a 3rd needle in the size your pattern calls for.

Tie the tails of your yarn into a slip knot and put the slip knot around the light tan needle. The knot does not count as the first stitch.

Hold the main color over the forefinger of your left hand and the contrasting color under your thumb. Use the other fingers of your left hand to secure the two working strands.

2 Because there is no loop of yarn to create the first stitch, you will need to start JMCO with step 4 to add a stitch of yellow yarn to the light tan needle (see page 14).

Then complete JMCO step 3 to add a blue stitch to the dark brown needle.

Repeat JMCO steps 4 and 3 until the number of stitches specified by your pattern have been cast on.

3 You will now begin double knitting using the 3rd needle. Hold the needles with the tips pointing to the left and the purl bump side up. Wrap the yellow yarn behind the blue yarn to secure the last blue stitch.

With both working strands behind the needles, knit the first blue stitch from the dark brown needle using the blue working yarn.

Move both working strands in front of the needles. Purl the first yellow stitch from the light tan needle using the yellow working yarn.

4 Continue knitting the blue stitches from the dark brown needle and purling the stitches from the light tan needle as specified in step 3 until all of the stitches have been worked.

Be careful to bring both strands to the back when knitting, and both strands to the front when purling. This prevents the yarn from being stranded across the outside of the work.

Once all of the stitches have been worked, return to your pattern instructions.

24

Laurel Jane's Cap

Laurel is my beloved second-born daughter, and at the age of five has a real love for hand knitted-items. This is the one cap my wee girl won't leave home without. Laurel adores the brim, the bright colors, and the diamond-shaped cables. I love that it meets my motherly standard for easy care: if it gets left out in a puddle, I just toss it in the washer and it's all good.

Deb Barnhill

Laurel Jane's Cap

Sizes
Small (medium, large)
Sized to fit a small child (bigger child, adult)
Brim circumference 16 (17.5, 19) inches
Stretches comfortably to at least 22 (24, 26) inches

Yarn
Brown Sheep Cotton Fleece [80% cotton, 20% merino wool; 215 yd/197 m per 100 g skein].

Version 1 (page 24):
  [MC] CW-365 Peridot; 1 skein
  [CC] CW-820 Teddy Bear; 1 skein

Version 2 (page 28):
  [MC] CW-725 Buttercream; 1 skein

Version 3 (page 27):
  [MC] CW-460 Jungle Green; 1 skein
  [CC] CW-840 Lime Light; 1 skein

Needles
2 US #5 [3.75 mm] 24-inch circular needles
—OR—
1 US #5 [3.75 mm] 32-inch – 40-inch circular needle
AND
1 US #5 [3.75 mm] 24-inch circular needle

Notions
2 stitch markers
Cable needle
Darning needle
One plastic placemat or plastic needlepoint canvas (optional - used to stiffen the brim)

Gauge
22 sts/32 rows = 4 inches in stockinette stitch

Substitutions
Any DK-weight cotton or cotton blend yarn.

Pattern Notes

This pattern is written to be worked on two circular needles for the brim and a single short circular needle for the body. The Magic Loop method or double-pointed needles may be substituted.

If you choose to work the body and brim in the same color, you can easily do so in any of the three sizes with a single skein.

T3b – Twist 3 back: Sl 1 to cn and hold in back; k2-tbl, p1 from cn.
T3f – Twist 3 front: Sl 2 to cn and hold in front; p1, k2 from cn tbl.
C4b – Cable 4 back: sSl 2 to cn and hold in back; k2, k2 from cn.
C4f – Cable 4 front: Sl 2 to cn and hold in front; k2, k2 from cn.
RLCinc – Right-leaning cable increase: Knit next 2 sts, but leave on LH needle; knit the same 2 sts again and pass to RH needle as usual--2 sts inc'd to 4 sts.
RLCdec – Right-leaning cable decrease: Sl 2 to cn and hold in back; [knit next st on LH needle tog with first st on cn] twice--4 sts dec'd to 2 sts.

Instructions

Brim

Using CC and Judy's Magic Cast on, CO 42 (48, 54) sts onto each of 2 circular needles—84 (96, 108) sts total.

Work first surface of brim on Needle 1 as follows:

Row 1 (RS): K16 [18, 20], M1R, pm, k10 (12, 14), pm, M1L, k2, turn—44 (50, 56) sts.
Row 2 (WS): Sl 1p wyif, p15 (17, 19), turn.
Row 3: Sl 1 pwise wyib, k to marker, M1R, sm, k to second marker, sm, M1L, k to 2 sts past gap created by previous row, turn.
Row 4: Sl 1p wyif, p to 2 sts past gap created by previous row, turn.

Repeat [Rows 3 and 4] 6 (7, 8) more times. All held sts have now been worked—58 (66, 74) sts on Needle 1. Do not break yarn.

Turn work so that WS is facing and, using working yarn, k across the 42 (48, 54) sts on Needle 2. Turn.

Using Needle 2, work second surface of brim as for first surface—58 (66, 74) sts on each needle.

Optional to stiffen brim: place folded brim on a plastic placemat, trace the outline and cut it out. Cut off point from each end so it won't poke through fabric. Exact size and shape are not critical, and the plastic doesn't need to fill the knitted brim completely.

Laurel Jane's Cap

Break yarn, leaving a 1.5 yd tail. With WS facing, graft sts of Needles 1 and 2 tog using Kitchener stitch, holding optional stiffener to the inside of the brim.

Hat body

Using one circular needle and MC, pick up and k 44 (50, 56) sts along folded edge of brim (1 st at each end and 1 st in each purl bump along folded surface).

Turn work so WS is facing and, using cable method, CO 32 (34, 36) sts. Turn work so RS is facing and join in round. K 2 (1, 0) st from brim and pm to indicate beg of rnd—76 (84, 92) sts.

Note: The first time that Chart A is work, K the 1st 2 and last 2 sts of Rnd 15. Do not move BOR marker.

Rnd 1: [P3, RLCinc, p3] 5 (6, 7) times, pm; k1, p1; *k2, p1; rep from * to last st, k1—86 (96, 106) sts.

Rnds 2 – 7: Work [Chart A Rnds 8–13] to marker, sm, work in rib as set to end.

Rnd 8: Work Chart A Rnd 14 as follows: Do not move marker; *k2, p6, k2; rep from * to marker, sm, work in rib as set to end of rnd.

Rnd 9: Work Chart A Rnd 15 as follows: k2, *p6, C4f; rep from * to 8 sts before marker, p6, k2, sm, work in rib as set to end of rnd.

Rnd 10: Work Chart A Rnd 16 as follows: Do not move marker; *k2, p6, k2; rep from * to marker, sm, work in rib as set to end of rnd.

Rnds 11 – 16: Work Chart A Rnds 1-6 to marker, sm, work in rib as set to end of rnd.

Rnd 17: Work Chart A Rnd 7 as set to marker, remove marker. *P1, pfb, RLCinc, pfb, p1; rep from * to end of rnd—110 (120, 130) sts.

Work Chart A Rnds 8–16, then Chart A Rnds 1–16 once more. Work measures about 5.5 inches from back CO edge.

Large size only:

Work Chart A Rnds 1–8 once more. Remove marker, p3, k2, replace marker. Work measures about 6.25 inches from back CO edge.

Crown Shaping
All sizes:

Work Chart B (decrease section), transferring work to 2 circular needles or double-point needles when needed—11 (12, 13) sts.

Final Rnd: K2tog 5 [6, 6] times, k 1 (0, 1)— 6 (6, 7) sts.

Break yarn and draw through rem sts. Bring to inside of work and fasten off. Weave in ends and block as desired.

Laurel Jane's Cap Version 3

Laurel Jane's Cap

Left: Laurel Jane's Cap Version 2
  Also shown: Eye Of The Needle, page 62

Below: Laurel Jane's Cap Version 1
  Also shown: Poncho Puzzle, page 136

Next page: Laurel Jane's Cap Version 3
  Also shown: Leaves A Fall'n, page 48

Laurel Jane's Cap

Cap Chart A

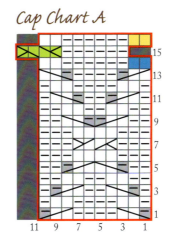

Cap Chart B

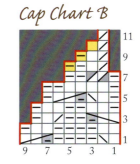

- ☐ Knit
- ⊟ Purl
- T3f (twist 3 front)
- T3b (twist 3 back)
- C4f (cable 4 front)
- C4b (cable 4 back)
- K2tog
- SSK
- ▢ Pattern rep
- ■ No st
- LCd (right-leaning cable dec)
- 🟩 On 1st rep of Chart A, k these sts do not cable
- 🟨 Move BOR marker to the right the number of sts shown; include sts in next rnd (omit 1st rep of Chart A)
- 🟦 Move BOR marker to the left the number of sts shown; include sts in current rnd (omit 1st rep of Chart A)

Hats ⚜ Beyond Toes

30

Haberdasher

I had knit several watch caps for my husband, ToolMan, from my handspun yarns. But he wanted a traditional golf, or driving cap. Knowing how the fabric caps of this kind are constructed, I thought about designing one that would be knit, with more shaping, with lining and an interior hatband to give it a more traditional, tailored appearance. With JMCO, it all clicked together; the construction problems I'd rolling around in my head were solved! And now, here it is for you. Enjoy!

Bobbie Wallace

Haberdasher

Finished Measurement
Circumference: 22 inches

Yarn
Hemp For Knitting Hempwol [65% wool, 35% hemp blend; 250 yd per 100 g skein]; 1 skein.

Version 1 (page 30):
Color: Terra
Version 2 (page 33):
Color: Scicilian Olive

Needles
One set US #4 [3.5 mm] double-point needles
2 US #4 [3.5 mm] 16-inch circular needles

Notions
Safety-pin type stitch markers. Note: Markers are placed on specific stitches, not needle cable, and must be removed later.
1 sheet plastic needlepoint canvas. A 9.25 inch circle works well.
1 fat quarter of fabric for lining, or piece approximately 18 inches x 21 inches
1 yd cotton double fold bias tape 1 inch wide
1 yd 3/4-inch non-roll woven elastic
Sewing thread to match fabric and bias tape
1 No. 2/0 sew-on snap

Gauge
24 sts/34 rows = 4 inches in St st

Substitutions
Blue Moon Fiber Arts Twisted; Cascade 220; any tweedy yarns that will make gauge

Pattern Notes
Read the entire pattern before beginning your project to understand the special construction and finishing used in this pattern.

Slip the first stitch of each row purlwise to create selvedge edge on all pieces.

Hat is worked in stockinette stitch.

Steam blocking is recommended. Crown will need to be blocked in two parts; once for crown and once for back shaping using a rolled towel to support crown section. Do not block crown back into a flat shape.

Pattern pieces for the lining are included. Copy all three pieces with 154% enlargement and use the enlarged pieces when cutting the lining and brim.

Instructions

Crown:
Using two 16-inch circular needles and JMCO, CO 45 sts to each needle—90 sts total.

Crown Back:
Working across top needle only (see instructions for "Knitting From Both Directions—Provisional Bay" on page 16): Slipping first st of each row, work flat in St st until piece measures 1.5 inches from cast-on.

Begin short-row shaping for crown back:
Row 1: K43, w&t.
Row 2: P42, w&t.
Row 3: K to within 1 st of last wrapped st, w&t.
Row 4: P to within 1 st of last wrapped st, w&t.
Rows 5 – 20: Rep [Rows 3 and 4] 8 times—10 wrapped stitches on each side and 25 unwrapped stitches in the center.

Place a safety-pin maker on both outside edges of the last row. The pins mark the corner of the crown/back where the side attaches.

Row 21: K25, k10, picking up wraps and knitting them with each st as you come to them.
Row 22: Sl 1, p34, p10 picking up wraps and purling them with each stitch as you come to them.

Continue working in St st as established for 2 inches from last short row worked (marked with safety-pin markers), slipping the first st of each row and ending with a WS row.

Begin back shaping:
Row 1 (RS): Sl 1, k2, KLL, k17, ssk, k1, k2tog, k17, KRL, k3, turn.
Row 2: P45, turn.

Haberdasher

Rows 3 – 10: [Rep rows 1 and 2] 4 more times. Place safety-pin marker at center and both sides of last row. The outside pins mark the corner where the back attaches to the side. The center pin marks the center back of the hat.

BO with RS facing, leaving markers in place.

Crown Front:
The crown front will be worked on the 45 resting sts from the second half of JMCO. Attach yarn and begin knitting on the RS of the piece.

Row 1 (RS): Sl 1, k44, turn.
Row 2: Sl 1, p44, turn.

Rep Rows 1 and 2 until piece measures 6 inches from cast-on (10 inches from safety pin marker on last short row at crown back), ending with a WS row.

Begin front shaping:
Row 1 (RS): Sl 1, k2, ssk, k35, k2tog, k3—43 sts.
Row 2: Sl 1, p42.
Row 3: Sl 1, k2, ssk, k33, k2tog, k3—41 sts.
Row 4: Sl 1, p40.
Row 5: Sl 1, k2, ssk, k31, k2tog, k3—39 sts.
Row 6: Sl 1, p38.
Row 7: Sl 1, k2, ssk, k29, k2tog, k3—37 sts.
Row 8: Sl 1, p36.
Row 9: Sl 1, k2, ssk, k27, k2tog, k3—35 sts.

Haberdasher, version 2
Also shown: November Street, page 120; Monica's Seaman's Scarf, page 69
Shawl pin: Tiggywinkle & Toolman

Haberdasher

Haberdasher, version 2;
Also shown: Monica's Seaman's Scarf, page 69

Row 10: Sl 1, p16, p1 placing center-of-crown marker on this st, p17, turn.
BO on RS, leaving marker in place.

Front/Sides:

The front and sides of the cap are worked in sections of short rows that provide shaping.

Using two 16-inch circular needles and JMCO, CO 23 st on each needle—46 sts total. Leave sts on second needle to be worked later. Place markers at each end of the JMCO and leave the markers in place as you proceed.

Left Front/Side:

Beginning with a RS row, work 3 rows St st.

Short-row shaping: *P13, w&t; K13, turn; p23, (hiding wrap on 13th st), turn; K23, turn; rep from * twice more and work last knit row as follows: K23, KRL, k1—24 stitches.

Work 2 rows St st.

Sort-row shaping: *P13, w&t; K13, turn; p23 (hiding wrap on 13th st), turn; work 5 rows in st st; rep from * once more and work last knit row as follows: k22, KRL, k1—25 stitches.

Work st st for 1 inch, ending on RS.

Short-row shaping: P13, w&t; k13, turn; p25 (hiding wrap on 13th st), turn.

Work St st 1.5 inches, ending with a WS row.
Next row (RS): K24, KRL, k1—26 sts.
Work stockinette for 1 inch, ending on WS.

Dec rows: *K to last 3 sts, k2tog, k1, turn; P to end, turn; rep from * twice more—23 sts.

K 1 row, turn.

Short-row shaping: *P13, w&t; K13, turn; p to end (hiding wrap on 13th st), turn; work 4 rows in St st; k to last 3 sts, k2tog, k1, turn; rep from * twice more, then p 1 row—20 stitches.

Place safety-pin marker on first st. BO 5 sts, k across to last 3 sts, k2tog, k1, turn.

Place safety-pin marker on first st.
P across, turn.

BO, leaving marker in place.

Right Front/Side:

Note: the right side is worked as for the left side, with shaping reversed.

Beginning on WS, work 3 rows St st, ending on WS.

Short-row shaping: *K13, w&t; p13, turn; k23 (hiding wrap on 13th st), turn; p23, turn; rep from * twice more and work last knit row as follows: k 1, KLL, k22—24 sts.

Work 2 rows St st.

Short-row shaping: *K13, w&t; p13, turn; k23 (hiding wrap on 13th st), turn; work 5 rows in St st; once more and work last knit row as follows: k1, KLL, k23—25 stitches.

Work St st for 1 inch, ending on WS.

Short-row shaping: K13, w&t; p13, turn; k25 (hiding wrap on 13th st), turn.

Haberdasher

Work in St st for 1.5 inches ending with a RS row and working last rows as follows: K1, KLL, k24—26 stitches.

Work in St st for 1 inch, ending on a RS row.
Dec rows: [P to last 3 sts, p2tog, p1, turn; k to end, turn] 3 times—23 sts.

P 1 row.

Short-row shaping: *K13, w&t; p13, turn; k to end (hiding wrap on 13th st), turn; work 4 rows in St st; p to last 3 sts, p2tog, p1, turn; rep from * twice more, then k one row—20 stitches.

Place safety-pin marker on first st. BO 5 sts, p across to last 3 sts, p2tog, p1, turn. Place safety-pin marker on first st. K across, turn.

BO, leaving marker in place.

Brim:
Using 2 16-inch circular needles and JMCO, CO 20 st to each needle—40 sts total.

Rnd 1: Knit around.
Rnd 2: Needle 1: K1, KLL, k to last st, KRL, k1. Needle 2: K1, KLL, k to last st, KRL, k1.

Rep [Rnds 1 and 2] 9 more times—40 sts on each needle; 80 sts total.

Begin side brim shaping:
Note: The shaping is worked at each side of the brim. You will be shifting sts on the needles during the Set-up row and then working flat.

Setup Row: K14, BO 6, place center-of-brim marker on last bound-off st, BO 6 leaving marker in place, k28, turn. Put these 28 sts on one needle; leave remaining stitches on other needle.

Side Of Brim:
Row 1: P28.
Row 2: K1, k2tog, knit to last 3 sts, ssk, k1.
Row 3: Purl across.
Rows 4–9: Rep [Rows 2 and 3] 3 more times—20 sts.
Row 10: K1, [k2tog] twice, k to last 5 sts, [ssk] twice, k1—16 sts.
Row 11: P across.
Rows 12–15: Rep [Rows 10 and 11] twice more—8 sts. BO.

Returning to sts on other needle. Attach yarn and begin working on RS.

BO 6, place center-of-brim marker on last bound-off st, BO 6 leaving marker in place. K28, turn.

Repeat Side Of Brim instructions for second side of brim.

Finishing
Match center marker of front/side piece to marker at center front of crown and markers at end of sides to markers on sides of crown back.

Sew sides to crown, using overcast stitch and being sure to catch both sides of selvedge sts; easing around curves to fit.

Brim:
Copy the brim pattern piece with 154% enlargement and use the enlarged piece when cutting the brim.

Haberdasher, version 1

Haberdasher

Haberdasher, version 1; also shown: Djinn, page 107

Cut plastic canvas according to pattern. Sew knitted brim over canvas, matching center markers and working from center to outside edges. Plastic canvas will bow slightly. Match center of brim to marked center of front/side. Using overcast stitch, sew brim to bottom edge of Front/Side, making sure brim is centered.

I-cord trim: Using 1 set double-point needles, CO 3 sts, [sl sts to other end of needle, k3] rep until I-cord measures 1 inch.

Begin applied I-cord: Starting at left side of brim and working around the outside of the hat opening, *pick up 1 st at edge using needle holding I-cord sts, sl sts to other end of needle, k2, k2tog (I-cord st and picked-up st); rep from * working around cap to opposite edge of brim and taking care not to stretch or gather edge.

Work free I-cord until I-cord is long enough to cover front seam, about 8 inches. BO. Sew loose I-cord to inside of brim, hiding seam. Graft ends of I-cord together at edge of brim.

Lining:

Copy lining pattern pieces with 154% enlargement and use the enlarged pieces when cutting the lining.

Pre-wash fabric, if necessary. Iron fabric. Fold in half; your folded fabric should measure about 18 inches x 11 inches. Using pattern, cut one side/front piece on the fold; cut one crown piece from the remaining fabric.

Mark center fronts and backs on both pieces. Machine baste 3/8 inch around both pieces. Clip curves and gather fabric so that pieces fit together, matching center front stars and back dots. Using 1/2-inch seams sew the outside curve of the Front/Side to the Crown/Back as for knitted pieces.

Turn knitted cap inside out. With wrong sides facing, loosely tack lining seams to knitted cap seams at several places around top and at the bottom of the back seams. Fold up 1/2 inch hem on fabric lining. Fold lining down over knitted cap. Using whipstitch (or catchstitch) sew bottom edge of lining to knitted cap just above I-cord around brim.

Hatband:

Cut a piece of elastic 23 inches long. Overlap ends by 1/2 inch and sew securely together, being careful not to twist.

Haberdasher

Cut a piece of bias tape 25 inches long. Encase elastic in fold of bias tape. Fold raw end of bias tape under ¼ inch, tack in place.

Divide hatband into quarters. On hat, mark points half-way between center front and center back. Pin hatband into hat, matching marks.

Using catchstitch or whipstitch, sew hatband into hat, catching threads from hat, lining, and both layers of hatband in each stitch.

Shaping:
Remove all markers. Steam cap, beginning with lining and moving to outside of cap, folding and shaping as you go. Plastic bags may be used to shape cap until dry. When dry, sew one part of snap to center front seam at crown and other to brim.

Wear in good health and enjoy the compliments!

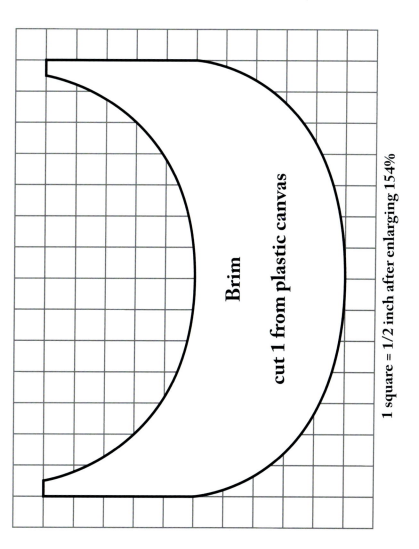

Brim
cut 1 from plastic canvas

1 square = 1/2 inch after enlarging 154%

Haberdasher

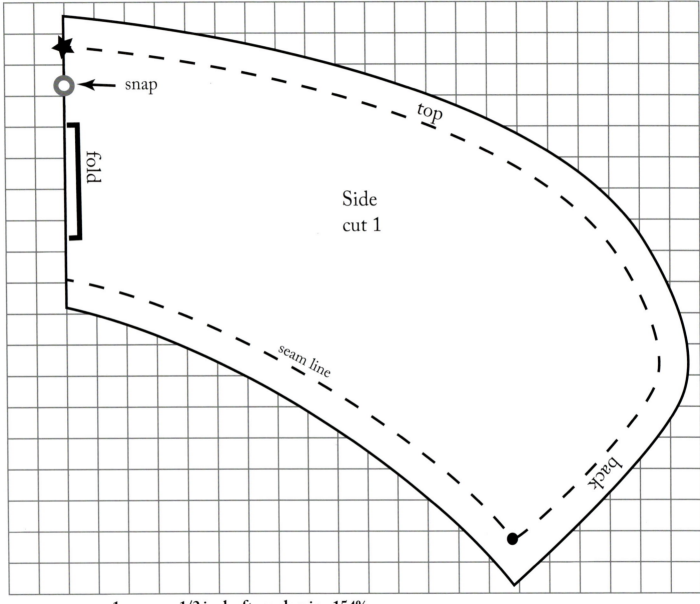

1 square = 1/2 inch after enlarging 154%

Beyond Toes & Hats

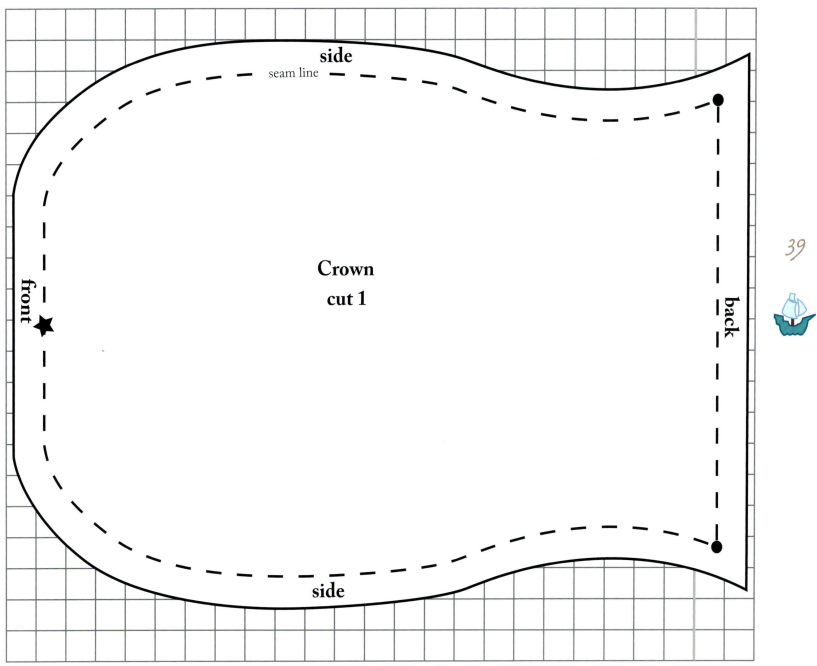

40

Charlie's Creature Cap

Playing with sock toe increase placement long ago, I discovered that if the increases are lined up as they are in this hat, you get very nice ears. When my grandson Charlie was born, I used this trick to knit him a creature cap, which you see here. It also has earflaps with whiskers at the ends.

Charlie's Creature Cap is sized for both children and adults, and makes a great Mom and child matched set, or Dad and child, or Mom, Dad, and children. Or anybody, really!

Cat Bordhi

Charlie's Creature Cap

Sizes
child (adult)

Finished measurements
Circumference: 18 (22) inches
Depth: 6 (7) inches

Yarn
Version 1 (page 40):
Malabrigo Twist (100% pure baby merino wool; 3.5 oz per 150 yd skein); color: Olive, 1 skein

Version 2 (page 43):
Blue Moon De-Vine (100% merino wool; 225 yd per 8 oz skein); color: Chestnutty; 1 skein is enough to make both child and adult caps

Needles
2 US #11 [8 mm] 24-inch circular needles
OR
1 US #11 [8 mm] 36-inch circular needle

Notions
4 stitch markers in different colors to designate as A, B, C and D

Gauge
13 sts = 4 inches in St st

Substitutions
Bulky yarns with some twist and spring.

Instructions
Using JMCO and circular needle(s), cast on 15 (19) sts to each needle—30 (38) sts total.

Top of head and ears
Rnd 1: Knit 5 (6), pm A, p5 (7) pm B, k10 (12), pm C, p5 (7), pm D, k5 (6).
Rnd 2: Knit.
Rnd 3: Knit to A, M1, sl A, p to B, sl B, M1, k to C, M1, sl C, p to D, sl D, M1, k to end—34 (42) sts.

Rep [Rnds 2 and 3] 5 (6) more times—54 (66) sts.

Main Hat
Remove markers in next round.

Knit all rnds until hat measures 5.5 (6.5) inches from top of crown to brim, changing to 1 circular needle when there is enough ease around to allow it.

Final rnd: K 22 (28), place A, k23 (29), place B.

Earflap
Knit to A, remove A.

Row 1 (RS): Knit 14, w&t.
Row 2 (WS): Knit 14, w&t.
Row 3: Knit 13, w&t.
Row 4: Knit 12, w&t.
Row 5: Knit 11, w&t.
Row 6: Knit 10, w&t.
Row 7: Knit 9, w&t.
Row 8: Knit 8, w&t.
Row 9: Knit 7, w&t.
Row 10: Knit 6, w&t.
Row 11: Knit 5, w&t.
Row 12: Knit 4, w&t.
Row 13: Knit 3, w&t.
Row 14: Knit 2, w&t.
Row 15: Knit 1, w&t.
Row 16: W&t.
Row 17: K1, pick up and knit 1 st before next st, k1—3 sts.

Work free I-cord as follows: *k3; do not turn; sl 3 sts back to LH needle; rep from * until I-cord measures 3 inches. K3tog.

Cut tail.

Second earflap
Slide sts from tip to tip until both tips emerge at B, ready to work.

Attach yarn. Remove B, then rep Rows 1-17 as for first earflap.

I-cord edge
Note: to work one rnd of applied I-cord: K2, k2tog tbl (1 I-cord st with 1 st from edge of earflap), replace 3 sts on LH needle.

Work 3 inches of free I-cord. Work applied I-cord, starting with first st at base of I-cord of one earflap.

Charlie's Creature Cap

After first 8 rnds of applied I-cord, pick up 1 st before next st and work applied I-cord into it.

Continue working applied I-cord to 8 sts before next earflap's I-cord. Pick up and knit 1 st before next st and work applied I-cord into it.

Work applied I-cord into next 8 sts. Work 3 inches of free I-cord, cut tail. Repeat on other side of hat.

Finishing

Weave in all ends (you can weave I-cord ends into I-cord tube).

Sew the 3 adjacent I-cords together invisibly where they meet the tip of each earflap so the I-cords are joined at the base of the earflap, and hang freely below.

Above: Charlie's Creature Cap Version 1

Below: Charlie's Creature Cap Version 2. Also shown: Poncho Puzzle, page 136

44

Headbumps

Headbumps is a fun hat to knit. You build the "bumps" one at a time with short rows. The lower edge is added last, making it easy to adjust the fit. You can also choose from two different edges, ribbing or I-cord.

Gayle Roehm

Headbumps

Sizes:
Child's hat (adult hat)
Head circumference approximately 18 (20 inches)

Yarn
Version 1 (page 44):
Crystal Palace Mini Mochi [80% merino wool, 20% nylon; 180 m/195 yd per 50 g ball]; color blue/green/purple #108; 2 balls.

(Note: you can make two hats of either size from three balls.)

Version 2 (page 47):
Noro Kureyon Sock [70% Wool, 30% Nylon; 420 m per 100 g skein]; color green/brown/yellow/ivory/turquoise S164; 1 skein.

Needles
1 US #3 [3.25 mm] 16-inch circular needle or size needed to obtain gauge
1 US #3 [3.25 mm] 24-inch or 32-inch circular needle (used only for cast-on)
1 set US #3 [3.25 mm] double-pointed needles

Notions
1 stitch marker

Gauge
26 sts/36 rows = 4 inches in St st
One pattern repeat (one bump) is about 2.5 inches wide.

Substitutions
Other sock yarns are also suitable; those with long color repeats emphasize the modular nature of the bumps and produce a more interesting hat!

Pattern Note
The bumps are made with short rows, where you turn your work and purl back. If this annoys you, you may want to practice knitting back backward.

Instructions
With two circular needles and holding the 16-inch needle on top and the longer needle on the bottom, use JMCO to cast on 112 (128) sts to each needle—224 (236) sts total. Pull out the ends of the longer needle and let them hang; work from the 16-inch needle.

Place a marker for the beg of the rnd. Knit 2 rnds.

Begin bumps pattern:
Row 3: K15, turn.
Row 4: Yo, p13, turn.
Row 5: Yo, k12, turn.
Row 6: Yo, p11, turn.
Row 7: Yo, k10, turn.
Row 8: Yo, p9, turn.
Row 9: Yo, k8, turn.
Row 10: Yo, p7, turn.
Row 11: Yo, k6, turn.
Row 12: Yo, p5, turn.
Row 13: Yo, k4, turn.
Row 14: Yo, p3, turn.
Row 15: Yo, k3, [k2tog] 6 times (knitting each yo with the st next to it).

Rep [Rows 3–15] 6 (7) more times, making a total of 7 (8) bumps.

Rnd 16: K1, * ssk 6 times (joining a st to the yo next to it), k10, repeat from * 6 (7) times, ending k9.
Rnd 17: Knit around.
Rnd 18: K112 (128), remove marker, k8, replace marker.

First set of bumps complete.

Rows 19-31: Rep [Rows 3–15] 7 (8) more times.
Rnd 32: Rep Rnd 16.
Rnd 33: Knit around.
Rnd 34: Remove marker, knit 104 (120), replace marker.

Second set of bumps complete.

For child's hat:
Rep [Row 3 to Rnd 34] once more, then rep [Row 3 to Rnd 18] once—5 sets of bumps.

For adult hat:
Rep [Row 3 to Rnd 34] twice more—6 sets of bumps.

Shape crown:
Change to dpns when there are too few sts for the circular needle.

Headbumps

Rnd 1: *K12 (14), k2tog, rep from * 7 more times.
Rnd 2 and all even-numbered rnds: Knit around.
Rnd 3: * K11 (13), k2tog, rep from * 7 more times.

Continue in this manner, on each odd-numbered rnd working 1 fewer st before each k2tog, until 8 sts rem.

Pull yarn through all sts and fasten off.

Lower Edge:
You have a choice of ribbing or I-cord for the bottom of the hat.

Ribbing Edge:
Rejoin yarn and knit 1 rnd with the 16-inch needle, decreasing 12 (16) sts evenly around—100 (112) total sts.

[K1, p1] around for 10 rnds.

BO using Jeni's Surprisingly Stretchy Bind Off or other stretchy bind off.

I-Cord Edge:
Rejoin yarn. [K3, k2tog] around, dec the st count by about 20%, with a couple of sts leftover at the end of the rnd.

Using knitted-on method, CO 3 sts on LH needle. * K2, ssk, sl these 3 sts back onto left needle, rep from * until 3 sts rem. Graft last 3 sts to the first 3 sts of the I-cord.

To add a second rd of I-cord:
Pick up one leg of each of the sts from first rnd of I-cord. Rep I-cord instructions for the second rnd.

Finishing
Weave in ends. Block if desired.

Right: Headbumps, Version 2

Lower Left: Headbumps, Version 1 with I-cord Edge

Lower Right: Headbumps, Version 1 with Ribbing Edge

Hats ~ Beyond Toes

48

Leaves A Fall'n

I am always inspired by my favorite season—the fall. I've wanted to do a leaf color-work hat for a while but didn't really want to dive into intarsia yet. Then I discovered a lovely technique called double knitting. This allows you to create two layers of fabric with no floats since you work each color every other stitch. Plus this method has the added bonus of creating a reversible fabric.

The hat is knit in the round and is seamless except at the start point where there is a small hole which will be seamed up at the end. This hole allows you to thread the optional elastic to give you a snugger fit since the hat should not be too tight or it will distort the image.

Chris Church

Leaves A Fall'n

Sizes:
Adult S (M, L)

Finished Measurements:
Circumference: 19.5 (21.5, 23.5) inches
Length: 8 inches for all sizes

Yarn:
Abstract Fiber Hand Dyed Yarn Matisse [100% superwash Blue-Faced Leicester wool; 420 yd per 100 g skein]

Version 1 (page 48):
[MC] Butternut; 1 skein
[CC] Mousse; 1 skein

Version 2 (page 51):
[MC] Deep Lake; 1 skein
[CC] Birch; 1 skein

Needles:
3 US #2 [2.75 mm] 16-inch circular needles. Two of these needles are used for the cast-on
1 set of US #2 [2.75 mm] double-point needles (for the crown decreases)

Notions:
7 stitch markers – 1 unique to mark the end of the round (5 of the markers are optional)
Tapestry needle
1.33 yards of round cord elastic (optional)
Colorwork yarn guide thimble (optional)

Gauge:
23.75 sts/40 rows = 4 inches in Double Knitting in the round

Substitutions:
Malabrigo Yarn Sock, Zitron Trekking (XXL), or other fingering weight or sock yarn. Be sure to pick two colorways that contrast so the design is apparent.

Pattern Notes:

Pick a size that doesn't have too much negative ease or the pattern will distort. Instead of using negative ease to fit the hat on your head, use the optional elastic to thread a cord into your hat to help it fit snugly. A half to a full inch are acceptable amounts of negative ease.

Double knitting is a method of working two layers at the same time. When working in double knit you will be working 2 stitches [back and front] for each stitch referred to in the pattern instructions and shown on the chart.

The chart represents the RS of the fabric and signifies 2 stitches: the front being the charted color and the back is the opposite of the charted color. It's wise to mark the charted section every 10 stitches so as not to lose your place. This will actually work out to be 20 stitches between each marker since you will be working both layers of fabric.

For your double knitting swatch, Rnd 1 equals the cast-on round and Rnd 22 the bind off. When you are done, you should have a wrist cuff measuring 6.4 inches in circumference and 2.2 inches in height. Swatching will allow you to tell if your colors will work. It might look horrible while you are all up close and paying attention to every stitch, but once it is washed and blocked, it will show its true colors.

The cast-on is a modified Judy's Magic Cast-on using the MC and CC tied together. When setting up the needles for JMCO, loop the MC over the top needle and the CC on the bottom needle. If you do it opposite, you will end up reversing your MC and CC.

Yarn made from Blue-Faced Leicester wool tends to grow a lot. If you discover your project grew too much in blocking, pop it in the dryer to return it to a more normal size.

This hat can be worn with either side facing out, with the hat body either matching or contrasting with the crown.

Instructions

Set up: Double Knit
Following Steps 1 – 4 of "Double Knitting With JMCO—Double Straits" on page 22, and using two circular needles, cast on 116 (128, 140) to each needle with MC on the top needle and CC on the bottom needle—232 (256, 280) sts total.

Leaves A Fall'n

Place a knot about 6 inches from the ends (you will use this later to seam up the tiny seam you will create while doing the cast on). Place BOR marker. Join in the round, making sure not to twist the stitches.

Work 2 rnds in St st.

Next rnd: K 31 (37, 43), pm, k53, pm, k32 (38, 44).

Charted Section: Double Knit
Work the chart over the 53 sts between the stitch markers using the Double Knit method in St st.

Transition Section: Double Knit
Work 3 rnds in St st. Work 1 rnd in Double Knit in St st all in the MC.

All work will now be in the MC.

K2tog (the front layer stitch with the back layer stitch) around so that you have a total of 116 (128, 140) sts.

Crown:
Work for 1.5 inches in St st. If you desire a longer or shorter hat, this is the spot to add or subtract length.

Rnd 1: *K6, k2tog; rep from * to last 4 (0, 4) sts, k4 (0,4)—102 (112, 123) sts.
Rnds 2 – 4: K all.
Rnd 5: *K4 (5, 4), k2tog; rep from * to last 0 (0, 3) sts, k0 (0, 3)—85 (96, 103) sts.
Rnds 6 – 8: K all.
Rnd 9: K1 (2, 2), k2tog, *k3 (4, 4), k2tog; repeat from * to last 2 (2, 3) sts, k2 (2, 3)—68 (80, 86) sts.
Rnds 10 – 12: K all.
Rnd 13: *K2, k2tog; rep from * to last 0 (0, 2) sts, k0 (0, 2)—51 (60, 65) sts.
Rnds 14 – 16: K all.
Rnd 17: K2tog, *k1, k2tog; rep from * to last 1 (1, 2) sts, k1 (1, 2)—34 (40, 44) sts.
Rnds 18 – 19: K all.
Rnd 20: K2tog around—17 (20, 22) sts.
Rnd 21: K all.
Rnd 22: K2tog around to last 0 (3, 0) sts, k3tog (0, k3tog)—8 (10, 10) sts.

Finishing:
Break yarn, thread through remaining 8 (10, 10) sts, and fasten. Block.

If the hat is a loose after blocking, thread the elastic onto a tapestry needle and pull it through the bottom hem of the hat using the small opening as your entry and exit point. Try on the hat and tension the elastic properly, tying a knot to lock it into the correct position. Hide the ends inside the hem.

Seam up the small hole with your cast-on tails. Weave in all ends.

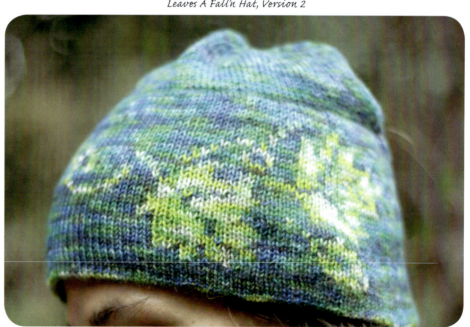

Leaves A Fall'n Hat, Version 2

Leaves A Fall'n

☐ With MC: (RS) K, (WS) P
■ With CC: (RS) K, (WS) P

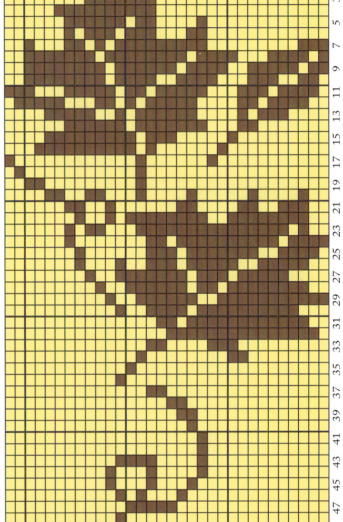

Leaves A Fall'n Swatch

Leaves A Fall'n Chart

Beyond Toes & Hats

54

Magic Cowl & Wristlet

Ask yourself a riddle… How do you go in two directions at once, and arrive at the same place at the same time? Why, with a double layered cowl, that's how!

This deliciously layered wristlet and cowl in two sizes and lengths are worked in the round in two opposing directions, beginning in the center with Judy's Magic Cast On. I have thought of making this type of layered scarf for a long time, but didn't have the tools to make it before Judy's brilliant revelation. Now it's easy and fun! Judy and I combined yarns and beads in four pretty ways… but I bet you can come up with lots more!

Sivia Harding

Magic Cowl & Wristlet

Sizes & Finished Measurements
Women's Wristlet (Small Cowl, Large Cowl)
Top Circumference: 7 (19.5, 19.5) inches
Bottom Circumference: 14 (27.5, 43.5) inches
Length: 7.25 (7, 11) inches

Yarn

Small Cowl Version 1 (page 59):

[MC] Curious Creek Fibers Omo [50% silk, 50% merino wool; 205 yd/187 m per 50 g skein]; color: Emerald City; 1 skein

[CC] Curious Creek Fibers Meru [51% wild tussah silk / 49% merino wool; 495 yd/450 m per 50 g skein]; color: Good Witch; 1 skein

Small Cowl Version 2 (page 59) and Wristlet (page 57):

[MC] Blue Moon Fiber Arts Seduction [50% merino, 50% tencel; 400 yd/366 m per 113 g skein]; color: Tanzanite; 2 skeins

[CC] Blue Moon Fiber Arts Silk Thread 2 [100% silk; 1,125 yd/1,028 m per 99 g skein]; color: Mossay; 1 skein

Large Cowl Version 1 (page 54):

[MC] Curious Creek Fibers Omo [50% silk, 50% merino wool; 205 yd/187 m per 50 g skein]; color: Plum Thunder; 1 skein

[CC] Curious Creek Fibers Meru [51% wild tussah silk, 49% merino wool; 495 yd/450 m per 50 g skein]; color: Birches of Norway; 1 skein

Large Cowl Version 2 (page 61):

[MC] Blue Moon Fiber Arts Seduction [50% merino, 50% tencel; 400 yd/ 366 m per 113 g skein]; color: Sunkissed Sand; 2 skeins

[CC] Blue Moon Fiber Arts Silk Thread 2 [100% silk; 1,125 yd/1,028 m per 99 g skein]; color: Meet Brown, Joe; 1 skein

Needles
2 US #5 [3.75 mm] 24-inch circular needles

Beads
112 (196, 392) size 8/0 or 6/0 seed beads, or equivalent

Small Cowl Version 1: 8/0 purple metallic iris Toho triangle beads, from Artbeads (www.artbeads.com)

Wristlet and Small Cowl Version 2: 4mm green iris megatama beads, from Artbeads (www.artbeads.com)

Large Cowl Version 1: 8/0 silver lined dark aqua beads, from Earthfaire (www.earthfaire.com)

Large Cowl Version 2: 8/0 Matte Apollo Toho triangle size beads, from Artbeads (www.artbeads.com)

Notions
Crochet hook, 0.6 mm (US 14)
Stitch markers
Yarn needle

Gauge
MC: 24 sts/30 rows = 4 inches in St st
21 sts/20 rows = 4 inches in pattern stitch (Large Border Pattern)
CC: 20 sts/34 rows = 4 inches in St st
19.5 sts/23 rows = 4 inches in pattern stitch (Large Border Pattern)

Substitutions
Any soft fingering weight yarn can be substituted for MC; any lace weight yarn can be substituted for CC.

If you substitute yarns, please check gauge carefully before you begin knitting.

Pattern Notes
Hooking Beads: perform the stitch or decrease indicated before you place the bead on the stitch. To do this, after working the stitch or decrease, transfer the stitch to the left needle, hook the bead on the stitch, then return the stitch to the right needle.

For each lace pattern, follow either the written instructions found on page 58, or the charts on page 60.

Instructions
Using JMCO with MC, cast on 32 (112, 112) sts on each needle—64 (224, 224) sts total.

Knit 2 rnds.

Bottom Layer
Using Needle 1 only and the 32 (112, 112) sts on that needle, join in the Rnd with knit side facing, meanwhile holding the other 32 (112, 112) sts on Needle 2.

You can move the sts on Needle 2 to a needle holder or piece of waste yarn if you prefer.

Purl 2 rnds on Needle 1.

Note: For Wristlet, you may choose to either use a needle with a small circumference, 2 circulars or the magic loop technique in order to work this small number of stitches comfortably in the round.

Magic Cowl & Wristlet

Wristlet:
Knit 13 rnds.
Work Rnds 1-32 of Body Expansion Pattern.
Work Rnds 1-10 of Border Lace Pattern.
BO loosely in knit.

Small Cowl:
Knit 42 rnds.
Work Rnds 1-10 of Border Lace Pattern.
BO loosely in knit.

Large Cowl:
Knit 42 rnds.
Work Rnds 1-32 of Body Expansion Pattern.
Work Rnds 1-10 of Border Lace Pattern.
BO loosely in knit.

Top Layer

All versions: Returning to Needle 2, join second set of 32 (112, 112) sts in the round with purl side facing.
Using CC, knit 2 rnds.

Wristlet:
Work Rnds 1-32 of Body Expansion Pattern.
Work Rnds 1-10 of Border Lace pattern.
BO loosely in knit.

Small Cowl:
Work Rnds 1-15 of Fern Lace Pattern.
Work Rnds 1-2 of Body Pattern 7 times, or 14 rnds total.
Work Rnds 1-10 of Border Lace Pattern.
BO loosely in knit.

Large Cowl:
Work Rnds 1-15 of Fern Lace Pattern.
Work Rnds 1-2 of Body Pattern 7 times, or 14 rnds total.
Work Rnds 1-32 of Body Expansion Pattern.
Work Rnds 1-10 of Border Lace Pattern.
BO loosely in knit.

Finishing

Close any gaps invisibly and weave in all ends. Immerse in lukewarm water, gently roll in a towel to dry, and pat out to shape.

Separate the layers and pin out lace points on both layers. The Version 1 picture on page 61 shows the bottom layer pulled longer than the top; the Version 2 picture shows the top layer pulled longer than the bottom.

Shape cowl around a rolled up towel or towels when half dry to prevent folds from appearing in your finished piece.

Below: Wristlets

Magic Cowl & Wristlet

Fern Lace Pattern
Over 16 sts, in rnds.
Rnd 1: K6, k2tog, yo, k6, k2tog, yo.
Rnd 2: Knit.
Rnd 3: Yo, ssk, k3, k2tog, yo, k1, yo, ssk, k3, k2tog, yo, k1.
Rnd 4: K to 1 st before EOR. Move BOR marker to this point.
Rnd 5: Ssk, yo, ssk, k1, k2tog, yo, k3, yo, ssk, k1, k2tog, yo, k1, yo.
Rnd 6: Knit.
Rnd 7: [Yo, ssk] twice, k2, yo, CDD, yo, k2, [k2tog, yo] twice, k1.
Rnd 8: K3, yo, ssk, k5, k2tog, yo, k4.
Rnd 9: K1, [yo, ssk, k1] twice, yo, ssk, k2tog, yo, k1, [k2tog, yo] twice.
Rnd 10: K2, [yo, ssk, k1] twice, k2tog, yo, k1, k2tog, yo, k3.
Rnd 11: [Yo, ssk, k1] twice, yo, CDD, yo, [k1, k2tog, yo] twice, k1.
Rnd 12: K1, yo, ssk, k1, yo, ssk, k3, k2tog, yo, k1, k2tog,yo, k2. On last repeat, end k1. Move BOR marker to this point.
Rnd 13: Ssk, k1, yo, ssk, k7, k2tog, yo, k2, yo.
Rnd 14: Ssk, k11, k2tog, yo, k1, yo.
Rnd 15: Knit.

Body Lace Pattern
Over 16 sts, in rounds
Rnd 1: K5, yo, CDD, yo, k8.
Rnd 2: Knit.

Rep Rnds 1 & 2 for patt.

Body Expansion Pattern
Over 16 sts increased to 32 sts, in rounds.
Rnd 1: K5, yo, CDD, yo, k6, yo, k1, yo, k1—18 sts.
Rnd 2 and all even numbered Rnds: Knit.
Rnd 3: K5, yo, CDD, yo, k5, k2tog, yo, k1, yo, ssk.
Rnd 5: K5, yo, CDD, yo, k7, yo, k1, yo, k2—20 sts.
Rnd 7: K5, yo, CDD, yo, k6, k2tog, yo, k1, yo, ssk, k1.
Rnd 9: K5, yo, CDD, yo, k8, yo, k1, yo, k3—22 sts.
Rnd 11: K5, yo, CDD, yo, k7, k2tog, yo, k1, yo, ssk, k2.
Rnd 13: K5, yo, CDD, yo, k9, yo, k1, yo k4—24 sts.
Rnd 15: K5, yo, CDD, yo, k8, k2tog, yo, k1, yo, ssk, k3.
Rnd 17: K5, yo, CDD, yo, k10, yo, k1, yo, k5—26 sts.
Rnd 19: K5, yo, CDD, yo, k9, k2tog, yo, k1, yo, ssk, k4.
Rnd 21: K5, yo, CDD, yo, k11, yo, k1, yo, k6—28 sts.
Rnd 23: K5, yo, CDD, yo, k10, k2tog, yo, k1, yo, ssk, k5.
Rnd 25: K5, yo, CDD, yo, k13, yo, k1, yo, k7—30 sts.
Rnd 27: K5, yo, CDD, yo, k11, k2tog, yo, k1, yo, ssk, k6.
Rnd 29: K5, yo, CDD, yo, k14, yo, k1, yo, k8—32 sts.
Rnd 31: K5, yo, CDD, yo, k12, k2tog, yo, k1, yo, ssk, k7.
Rnd 32: Knit.

Border Lace Pattern
Over 16 sts increased to 22 sts, in rounds
Rnd 1: K5, yo, CDD B, yo, k8.
Rnd 2: Knit.
Rnd 3: K5, k1 B, yo, k1, yo, k1 B, k8—18 sts.
Rnd 4: Knit.
Rnd 5: K4, k2tog B, yo, k1, k1 B, k1, yo, ssk B, k7.
Rnd 6: Knit.
Rnd 7: K4, k1 B, yo, k1, yo, CDD B, yo, k1, yo, k1 B, k7—20 sts.
Rnd 8: Knit.
Rnd 9: K4, k1 B, yo, k1, k2tog B, yo, k1 B, yo, ssk B, k1, yo, k1 B, k7—22 sts.
Rnd 10: Purl.

Magic Cowl & Wristlet

Right: Small Cowl, Version 2

Below: Small Cowl, Version 1

Neckwear ~ Beyond Toes

Magic Cowl & Wristlet

Fern Lace Chart
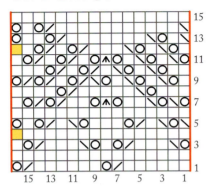

Body Lace Chart
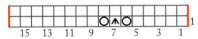

Expansion Lace Chart
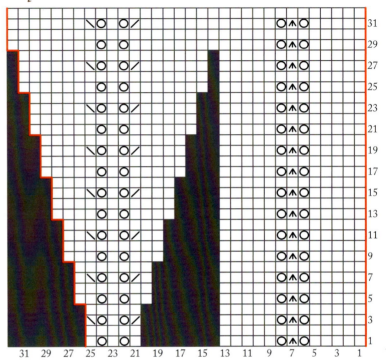

	Legend
☐	Knit
−	Purl
∕	K2tog
∖	SSK
⋏	CDD: Sl 2 tog, k1, pass 2 sl st over
▇ (green)	Place bead
▇ (yellow)	On the last repeat of the round only, do not work this stitch. Move the BOR marker to the right of this stitch and include this stitch in the next round.
○	Yo
▢	Pattern repeat
▇ (black)	No stitch

Border Lace Chart
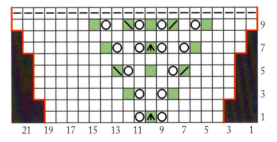

Beyond Toes ~ Neckwear

Magic Cowl & Wristlet

Right: Large Cowl, Version 1

Below: Large Cowl, Version 2

Neckwear — Beyond Toes

62

Eye Of The Needle

*I*nspired by the gigantic scarves seen consuming their wearers on the streets of Paris, often doubled upon themselves with the ends looped through, this cabled scarf matches the scale and warmth of its French brethren but without the bulk and length, resulting in a snug, cozy, dramatic piece knit with half the length.

The scarf resembles a needle with the JMCO edge worked into a loop upon itself to form the eye. A large reversible central cable continues the theme, creating more "eyes" where the fabric crosses over itself. Treat your neck to a luxury fiber in the weight of your choice. Pattern is written in two variations: longer with additional cable panels in Aran-weight yarn and a shorter, simpler version in bulky-weight yarn.

Stephen Houghton

Eye Of The Needle

Finished Measurements
60 inches x 9 inches in Aran weight yarn
34 inches x 8 inches in bulky weight yarn

Yarn
Aran Version 1 (page 62, right):
Blue Moon Fiber Arts Peru [50% alpaca/30% merino wool/20% silk; 500 yd/457 m per 8 oz/226 g skein]; color: Pond Scum; 1 skein

Aran Version 2 (page 62, left):
Blue Moon Fiber Arts Socks That Rock Heavyweight [100% superwash merino wool; 350 yds/320 m per 7 oz/198 g skein]; color: Stonewashed; 2 skeins

Bulky Version (page 65):
Blue Moon Fiber Arts De-Vine [100% merino wool; 225 yd/205 m per 8 oz/226 g skein]; color: Bleck; 1 skein

Needles
Aran
2 US #7 [4.5 mm] 20-inch (or longer) circular needles
Bulky
2 US #13 [9 mm] 20-inch (or longer) circular needles

Notions
Cable needle or 1 double-point needle in any size equal or smaller to project needle
Tapestry needle

Gauge
Aran
22 sts/24 rows = 4 inches in St st
Bulky
12 sts/16 rows = 4 inches in St st

Substitutions
Any yarn in Aran or bulky weight that you'd like against your neck.

Pattern Notes
Aran Cables:
2/1 LPC: Sl 2 to cn, hold to front, p1; k2 from cn.
2/1 RPC: Sl 1 to cn, hold to back, k2; p1 from cn.
2/1 LC: Sl 2 to cn, hold to front, k1; k2 from cn.
2/1 RC: Sl 1 to cn, hold to back, k2; k1 from cn.
11/1/11 cable: Sl 12 to cn (or spare dpn), hold to front; p2, k1, p2, k1, p2, k1, p2; slip leftmost st from cn back onto LH needle, k this st; p2, k1, p2, k1, p2, k1, p2 from cn.

Bulky Cable:
8/1/8 cable – Sl 9 to cn (or spare dpn), hold to front; p2, k1, p2, k1, p2; slip left-most st from cn back onto LH needle, k this st; p2, k1, p2, k1, p2 from cn.

Instructions - Bulky weight
Using two circular needles and Judy's Magic Cast-on, CO 35 sts onto each needle—70 sts total. Rotate needles 180-degrees to begin with working yarn on right and k sts facing. You'll be working on the top needle and the bottom needle will rest for now.

Row 1 (RS): Sl 1, p2, k4, p2, [k2, p1] 5 times, k2, p2, k4, p3.
Row 2 (WS): Sl 1, k2, p4, k2, [p2, k1] 5 times, p2, k2, p4, k3.
Repeat these two rows until piece measures 9.75 inches ending with Row 1.

Eye Of The Needle loop
Join the two ends of the scarf to form a loop as follows:
Hold the working needle and the needle with the resting cast-on sts parallel with right sides to the outside and the working needle in front.

Work 1 st from the front needle together with 1 st from the back needle in pattern: k2tog 3 times, p2tog 4 times, k2tog twice, [p2tog twice, k2tog] 5 times, p2tog twice, k2tog twice, p2tog 4 times, k2tog 3times.
Turn and work 1 row in patt: Sl 1, p2, k4, p2, [k2, p1] 5 times, k2, p2, k4, p3.

Length of scarf and cables
Row 1: Sl 1, k2, p4, k2, [p2, k1] 5 times, p2, k2, p4, k3.
Row 2: Sl 1, p2, k4, p2, [k2, p1] 5 times, k2, p2, k4, p3.
Rows 3-32: Rep [Rows 1 and 2] 15 more times.
Row 33: Sl 1, k2, p4, k2, 8/1/8 cable, k2, p4, k3.
Row 34: Rep Row 2.
Rep [Rows 1–34] twice more times—3 reps total.
Rep [Rows 1-16].

Eye Of The Needle

Finishing - tubular bind-off
Row 1: K2tog, p1, [k1, p1] 16 times.
Row 2: [K1, p1] 17 times.
Row 3: [K1, sl 1 wyif] 17 times.
Row 4: Rep Row 3.

Using a spare set of needles, separate sts onto 2 sets of needles by alternately slipping k sts onto front needle and p sts on to back needle. Each needle will hold 17 sts.

Cut yarn, leaving 36-inch tail. With embroidery needle, graft sts together with Kitchener stitch, as if closing the toe of a sock. Weave in ends. To maintain the bulky yarn's ropey effect, no blocking is necessary.

Instructions - Aran weight
Using two circular needles and Judy's Magic Cast-On, CO 57 sts onto each needle—114 sts total. Rotate needles 180-degrees to begin with working yarn on right and k sts facing. You'll be working with the sts on the top needle and the bottom needle will hibernate for now.

Row 1 (RS): Sl 1, k2, p2, k10, p2, [k2, p1] 7 times, k2, p2, k10, p2, k3.
Row 2 (WS): Sl 1, p2, k2, p10, k2, [p2, k1] 7 times, p2, k2, p10, k2, p3.

Rep these 2 rows until piece measures 9 inches, ending with Row 1.

Eye Of The Needle loop
Join the two ends of the scarf to form a loop as follows:

Hold the working needle and the needle with the resting cast-on sts parallel with right sides to the outside and the working needle in front.

Work 1 st from the front needle together with 1 st from the back needle in pattern: p3tog 3 times, k2tog twice, p2tog 10 times, k2tog twice, [p2tog twice, k2tog] 7 times, p2tog twice, k2tog twice, p2tog 10 times, k2tog twice, p2tog 3 times—57 sts.

Turn and work 1 row in patt: Sl 1, k2, p2, k10, p2, [k2, p1] 7 times, k2, p2, k10, p2, k3.

Length of scarf and cables
Begin Aran Scarf Main Chart on page 67, or follow the Aran Scarf Pattern written instructions below.

Rep [Rows 1–48] 6 times.

Finishing - tubular bind-off
Row 1: K2tog, p1, [k1, p1] 27 times—57 sts.
Row 2: [K1, p1] 28 times.
Row 3: [K1, sl 1 wyif] 28 times.
Rows 4-6: Rep Row 3.

Using a spare set of needles, separate sts onto 2 sets of needles by alternately slipping k sts onto front needle and p sts on to back needle. Each needle will hold 28 sts. Cut yarn, leaving 36-inch tail. With embroidery needle, graft sts together with Kitchener stitch. Weave in ends. Lightly block.

Aran Scarf Pattern
Row 1: Sl 1, p2, 2/1 LC, p9, k2, [p2, k1] 7 times, p2, k2, p9, 2/1 RC, p3.
Row 2: Sl 1, k2, p3, k9, p2, [k2, p1] 7 times, k2, p2, k9, p3, k3.
Row 3: Sl 1, p2, k1, 2/1 LC, p8, k2, [p2, k1] 7 times, p2, k2, p8, 2/1 RC, k1 p3.
Row 4: Sl 1, k2, p4, k8, p2, [k2, p1] 7 times, k2, p2, k8, p4, k3.
Row 5: Sl 1, p2, k2, 2/1 LPC, p7, k2, [p2, k1] 7 times, p2, k2, p7, 2/1 RPC, k2 p3.

Eye Of The Needle, Bulky Version

Eye Of The Needle

Row 6: Sl 1, k2, p2, k1, p2, k7, p2, [k2, p1] 7 times, k2, p2, k7, p2, k1, p2, k3.

Row 7: Sl 1, p2, k2, p1, 2/1 LPC, p6, k2, [p2, k1] 7 times, p2, k2, p6, 2/1 RPC, p1, k2, p3.

Row 8: Sl 1, k2, p2, k2, p2, k6, p2, [k2, p1] 7 times, k2, p2, k6, p2, k2, p2, k3.

Row 9: Sl 1, p2, k2, p2, 2/1 LPC, p5, k2, [p2, k1] 7 times, p2, k2, p5, 2/1 RPC, p2, k2, p3.

Row 10: Sl 1, k2, p2, k3, p2, k5, p2, [k2, p1] 7 times, k2, p2, k5, p2, k3, p2, k3.

Row 11: Sl 1, p2, k2, p3, 2/1 LPC, p4, k2, [p2, k1] 7 times, p2, k2, p4, 2/1 RPC, p3, k2, p3.

Row 12: Sl 1, k2, p2, k4, p2, k4, p2, [k2, p1] 7 times, k2, p2, k4, p2, k4, p2, k3.

Row 13: Sl 1, p2, 2/1 LC, p3, k2, p4, k2, 11/1/11 cable, k2, p4, k2, p3, 2/1 RC, p3.

Row 14: Sl 1, k2, p3, k3, p2, k4, p2, [k2, p1] 7 times, k2, p2, k4, p2, k3, p3, k3.

Row 15: Sl 1, p2, k1, 2/1 LC, p2, k2, p4, k2, [p2, k1] 7 times, p2, k2, p4, k2, p2, 2/1 RC, k1, p3.

Row 16: Sl 1, k2, p4, k2, p2, k4, p2, [k2, p1] 7 times, k2, p2, k4, p2, k2, p4, k3.

Row 17: Sl 1, p2, k2, 2/1 LPC, p1, k2, p4, k2, [p2, k1] 7 times, p2, k2, p4, k2, p1, 2/1 RPC, k2, p3.

Row 18: Sl 1, k2, p2, k1, p2, k1, p2, k4, p2, [k2, p1] 7 times, k2, p2, k4, p2, k1, p2, k1, p2, k3.

Row 19: Sl 1, p2, k2, p1, 2/1 LPC, k2, p4, k2, [p2, k1] 7 times, p2, k2, p4, k2, 2/1 RPC, p1, k2, p3.

Row 20: Sl 1, k2, p2, k2, p4, k4, p2, [k2, p1] 7 times, k2, p2, k4, p4, k2, p2, k3.

Row 21: Sl 1, p2, k2, p2, 2/1 LPC, k1, p4, k2, [p2, k1] 7 times, p2, k2, p4, k1, 2/1 RPC, p2, k2, p3.

Row 22: Sl 1, k2, p2, k3, p3, k4, p2, [k2, p1] 7 times, k2, p2, k4, p3, k3, p2, k3.

Row 23: Sl 1, p2, k2, p3, 2/1 LPC, p4, k2, [p2, k1] 7 times, p2, k2, p4, 2/1 RPC, p3, k2, p3.

Row 24: Sl 1, k2, p2, k4, p2, k4, p2, [k2, p1] 7 times, k2, p2, k4, p2, k4, p2, k3.

Row 25: Sl 1, p2, k2, p4, 2/1 LC, p3, k2, [p2, k1] 7 times, p2, k2, p3, 2/1 RC, p4, k2, p3.

Row 26: Sl 1, k2, p2, k4, p3, k3, p2, [k2, p1] 7 times, k2, p2, k3, p3, k4, p2, k3.

Row 27: Sl 1, p2, k2, p4, k1, 2/1 LC, p2, k2, [p2, k1] 7 times, p2, k2, p2, 2/1 RC, k1, p4, k2, p3.

Row 28: Sl 1, k2, p2, k4, p4, k2, p2, [k2, p1] 7 times, k2, p2, k2, p4, k4, p2, k3.

Row 29: Sl 1, p2, k2, p4, k2, 2/1 LPC, p1, k2, [p2, k1] 7 times, p2, k2, p1, 2/1 RPC, k2, p4, k2, p3.

Row 30: Sl 1, k2, p2, k4, p2, k1, p2, k1, p2, [k2, p1] 7 times, k2, p2, k1, p2, k1, p2, k4, p2, k3.

Row 31: Sl 1, p2, k2, p4, k2, p1, 2/1 LPC, k2, [p2, k1] 7 times, p2, k2, 2/1 RPC, p1, k2, p4, k2, p3.

Row 32: Sl 1, k2, p2, k4, p2, k2, p4, [k2, p1] 7 times, k2, p4, k2, p2, k4, p2, k3.

Row 33: Sl 1, p2, k2, p4, k2, p2, 2/1 LPC, k1, [p2, k1] 7 times, p2, k1, 2/1 RPC, p2, k2, p4, k2, p3.

Row 34: Sl 1, k2, p2, k4, p2, k3, p3, [k2, p1] 7 times, k2, p3, k3, p2, k4, p2, k3.

Row 35: Sl 1, p2, k2, p4, k2, p3, 2/1 LPC, [p2, k1] 7 times, p2, 2/1 RPC, p3, k2, p4, k2, p3.

Row 36: Sl 1, k2, p2, k4, p2, k4, p2, [k2, p1] 7 times, k2, p2, k4, p2, k4, p2, k3.

Row 37: Sl 1, p2, k2, p4, 2/1 LPC, p3, k2, [p2, k1] 7 times, p2, k2, p3, 2/1 RPC, p4, k2, p3.

Row 38: Sl 1, k2, p2, k5, p2, k3, p2, [k2, p1] 7 times, k2, p2, k3, p2, k5, p2, k3.

Row 39: Sl 1, p2, k2, p5, 2/1 LPC, p2, k2, [p2, k1] 7 times, p2, k2, p2, 2/1 RPC, p5, k2, p3.

Row 40: Sl 1, k2, p2, k6, p2, k2, p2, [k2, p1] 7 times, k2, p2, k2, p2, k6, p2, k3.

Row 41: Sl 1, p2, k2, p6, 2/1 LPC, p1, k2, [p2, k1] 7 times, p2, k2, p1, 2/1 RPC, p6, k2, p3.

Row 42: Sl 1, k2, p2, k7, p2, k1, p2, [k2, p1] 7 times, k2, p2, k1, p2, k7, p2, k3.

Row 43: Sl 1, p2, k2, p7, 2/1 LPC, k2, [p2, k1] 7 times, p2, k2, 2/1 RPC, p7, k2, p3.

Row 44: Sl 1, k2, p2, k8, p4, [k2, p1] 7 times, k2, p4, k8, p2, k3.

Row 45: Sl 1, p2, k2, p8, 2/1 LPC, k1, [p2, k1] 7 times, p2, k1, 2/1 RPC, p8, k2, p3.

Row 46: Sl 1, k2, p2, k9, p3, [k2, p1] 7 times, k2, p3, k9, p2, k3.

Row 47: Sl 1, p2, k2, p9, 2/1 LPC, [p2, k1] 7 times, p2, 2/1 RPC, p9, k2, p3.

Row 48: Sl 1, k2, p2, k10, p2, [k2, p1] 7 times, k2, p2, k10, p2, k3.

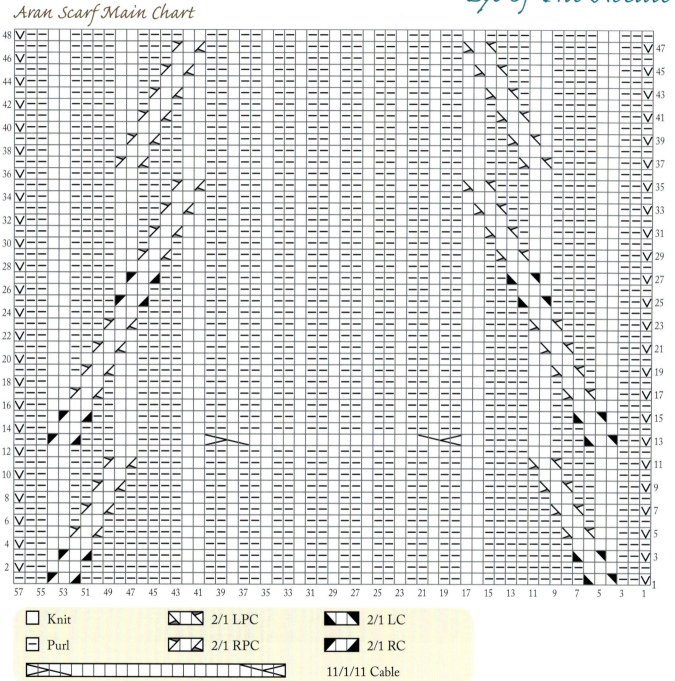

Eye Of The Needle

Aran Scarf Main Chart

- ☐ Knit
- ⊟ Purl
- ◨◧ 2/1 LPC
- ◩◪ 2/1 RPC
- ◨◧ 2/1 LC
- ◩◪ 2/1 RC
- 11/1/11 Cable

Neckwear ⚓ Beyond Toes

68

Monica's Seamen's Scarf

This lace scarf, with matching lace tails, uses the neckline ribbing characteristic of the scarves of the Seamen's Church Institute of New York and New Jersey. The scarf begins with JMCO. Half of the stitches are used for working the neckline ribbing and proceeding on to knitting one lace tail. The other half of the stitches are worked in the opposite direction for the other lace tail.

The scarf is named in honor of Monica Kullarand, a wonderful Estonian lace knitter. Monica and her son graciously hosted my husband and me on a wonderful visit to the Haapsalu Ratiku Museum in Estonia. The lace pattern stitch of this scarf is based on Tornikiri, from "The Haapsalu Shawl: A Knitted Lace Tradition from Estonia"[1] by Siiri Reimann and Aime Edasi.

Myrna A. I. Stahman

Monica's Seamen's Scarf

Finished Measurements
Width after blocking: 5.5 inches
Length, point to point: 45.5 inches
Neckline ribbing: 9.5 inches
Tail from neckline ribbing to point: 18 inches

Yarn
Buffalo Gold Heaven [100% pure bison down, 400 yd per 50 g skein]; less than one skein (finished scarf weighs just 24 grams [0.9 ounces])

Needles
One US #2 [3.0 mm] circular needle for the tails
One US #1.5 [2.75 mm] circular needle for the neckline ribbing

Notions
4 fine stitch markers for placement between the borders and the body of the lace tails (optional)

Gauge
The number of stitches and rows per inch are of minor importance when knitting a lace Seamen's scarf. What is important is that you are happy with the width of the scarf and the look and feel of the fabric produced.

Substitutions
The following Buffalo Gold yarns work great with this pattern: Myrna Stahman's Dream – Almost Cobweb; Lux; Earth; Moon; Moon Lite.
Almost any lace weight or fingering weight yarn may be used.

Pattern Notes
The stitches are cast on using the two different sizes of circular needles. The stitches on the smaller needle are used immediately for working the neckline ribbing. The stitches on the larger needle will be used when working the lace pattern.

After you have completed knitting the neckline ribbing, use the larger needle to knit the tails. Both tails may be knit at the same time, using two different balls or yarn. Or, you may knit one tail first and later knit the second tail.

Instructions
Using Judy's Magic Cast-On and smaller circular needle, cast 33 sts on to each needle—66 stitches total.

Neckline Ribbing
Working flat on Needle 1, work the 33 neckline ribbing sts as follows. The sts on Needle 2 will rest until the first tail is complete. After the first row or two they can be moved to a st holder or waste yarn if desired.
WS Rows: P6, k4, p3, k2, p3, k2, p3, k4, p6.
RS Rows: K6, p4, k3, p2, k3, p2, k3, p4, k6.

Work until the neckline ribbing measures approximately 70% of the circumference of the neck of the person for whom the scarf is being made, generally between 9 and 12 inches.

End after completing a WS Row.

First Tail
Using the larger needle, begin working the first tail. Follow either the written instructions on this page or the charted instructions on page 72.

Written Instructions:
"B6" (border sts) at the beginning of each row is worked as follows: With the yarn in front of your work, slip the first stitch as if to purl, pass the yarn between the points of your needles to the back of your work, k1, p1, k1, p1, k1.
B6 (border sts) at the end of each row is worked as follows: K1, p1, k1, p1, k2.

Note: The first time that [Rows 1-32] are worked, knit the first st on Row 1 instead of slipping it. On all other repeats of [Rows 1-32], slip the first st on Row 1.

Rows 1, 3, 5, & 7 (RS): B6, [k1, ssk, k2, yo, k1, yo, k2, k2tog] 2 times, k1, B6—33 sts.
Row 2 and all even-numbered rows (WS): B6, p 21, B6.
Row 9: B6, [k1, yo, ssk, k5, k2tog, yo] 2 times, k1, B6.
Row 11: B6, [k2, yo, ssk, k3, k2tog, yo, k1] 2 times, k1, B6.
Row 13: B6, [k3, yo, ssk, k1, k2tog, yo, k2] 2 times, k1, B6.
Row 15: B6, [k4, yo, sk2p, yo, k3] 2 times, k1, B6.

Monica's Seamen's Scarf

Rows 17, 19, 21 & 23: B6, [k1, yo, k2, k2tog, k1, ssk, k2, yo] 2 times, k1, B6.
Row 25: B6, [k3, k2tog, yo, k1, yo, ssk, k2] 2 times, k1, B6.
Row 27: B6, [k2, k2tog, yo, k3, yo, ssk, k1] 2 times, k1, B6.
Row 29: B6, [k1, k2tog, yo, k5, yo, ssk] 2 times, l1. B6.
Row 31: B6, k2tog, yo, k7, yo, sk2p, yo, k7, yo, ssk, B6.
Row 32: Purl.

Repeat [Rows 1-32] 3 times.

Repeat [Rows 1-16] once more, then work the following rows for shaping the point of the tail:

Row 1: B6, ssk, k4, ssk, k2, yo, k1, yo, k2, k2tog, k4, k2tog, B6—31 sts.
Row 3: B6, ssk, k3, ssk, k2, yo, k1, yo, k2, k2tog, k3, k2tog, B6—29 sts.
Row 5: B6, ssk, k2, ssk, k2, yo, k1, yo, k2, k2tog, k2, k2tog, B6—27 sts.
Row 7: B6, ssk, k1, ssk, k2, yo, k1, yo, k2, k2tog, k1, k2tog, B6—25 sts.
Row 9: B6, ssk, yo, ssk, k5, k2tog, yo, k2tog, B6—23 sts.
Row 11: B6, ssk, yo, ssk, k3, k2tog, yo, k2tog, B6—21 sts.
Row 13: B6, ssk, yo, ssk, k1, k2tog, yo, k2tog, B6—19 sts.
Row 15: B6, ssk, yo, sk2p, yo, k2tog, B6—17 sts.
Row 17: B6, ssk, k1, k2tog, B6—15 sts.
Row 19: B6, sk2p, B6—13 sts.

Neckwear ~ Beyond Toes

Monica's Seamen's Scarf

Row 20: Sl 1, k1, p1, k1, p5, k1, p1, k2—13 sts.
Row 21: Sl 1, k1, p1, k1, p1, sk2p, p1, k1, p1, k2—11 sts.
Row 22: Sl 1, [k1, p1] 4 times, k2—11 sts.
Row 23: Sl 1, k1, p1, k1, p3tog, k1, p1, k2—9 sts.
Row 24: Sl 1, [k1, p1] 3 times, k2—9 sts.
Row 25: Sl 1, k1, p1, sk2p, p1, k2—7 sts.
Row 26: Sl 1, [k1, p1] 2 times, k2—7 sts.
Row 27: Sl 1, k1, p3tog, k2—5 sts.
Row 28: Sl 1, k1, p1, k2—5 sts.
Row 29: Sl 1, p3tog, k1—3 sts.
Row 30: Sl, p1, k1—3 sts.
Row 31: CDD, cut the yarn, and pull the end of the yarn through the last st.

Attach the yarn on the RS of Needle 2. Work the second tail as for the first tail.

Chart Instructions

Note: The first time that Chart A is worked, knit the first st on Row 1 instead of slipping it. On all other repeats of Chart A, slip the first st on Row 1.

Both RS and WS rows are shown on Charts A, C, and E.
Only RS rows are shown on Charts B and D. All WS rows on Charts B and D are purled.
Charts A and C repeat 16 times for every 1 repeat of Charts B.
Charts A and C repeat 20 times for every 1 repeat of Chart D.

Work Row 1 of Chart A (right border), pm, work the first row of Chart B (lace pattern), pm, work Row 1 of Chart C (left border), turn.

Work Row 2 of Chart C, sm, purl to marker, sm, work Row 2 of Chart A, turn.

Continue until Chart B has been worked 3 times.

Continue, working Rows 1–16 of Chart B one more time.
Work Row 1 of Chart A, sm, Row 1 of Chart D, sm, Row 1 of Chart C, turn.
Work Row 2 of Chart C, sm, purl to marker, sm, work Row 2 of Chart A, turn.
Continue until all rows of Chart D have been work, ending with Row 19 (RS).

Work all rows of Chart E.

Break off yarn and attach on RS of Needle 2.

Second Tail

Work as for first tail.

Finishing

Weave in all ends.

Carefully wash your beautiful Seamen's scarf.

Block your scarf, using blocking wires and T-pins on the edges of the tail, but not on the neckline ribbing. Let thoroughly dry.

*Shawl Pin: Tiggywinkle & Toolman
Also shown: Bobsled Mittens, page 80*

Beyond Toes — Neckwear

Monica's Seamen's Scarf

- ☐ K on RS; p on WS
- ⊟ P on RS; k on WS
- ╱ K2tog
- ╲ SSK
- ◯ Yo
- ⊻ Sl 1 pwise with yarn held to front of work
- ⋀ CDD: Sl 2 tog kwise, k1, p2sso
- P3tog
- Sk2p: Sl 1, k2tog, psso
- ▭ Pattern repeat
- ▪ No stitch

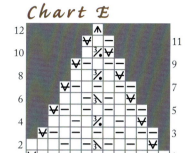

Chart E

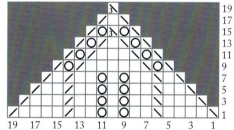

Chart D

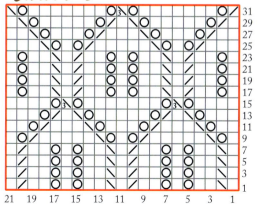

Chart B

Chart C

Chart A

Neckwear — Beyond Toes

Swept Off My Feet

It will come as no surprise that I love to knit socks. Swept Off My Feet indulges a sock passion in the form of a warm wrap for your neck.

If you have not knit socks before, this pattern is a fun way to try out sock construction. Because there's no need to fit these socks to someone's foot, gauge is unimportant. The size of the scarf will vary depending on the yarn and needles you choose. The feet can point the same direction, or opposite directions. Have fun making this scarf your own!

Judy Becker

Swept Off My Feet

Finished Measurements
Approximately 60 inches long x 5 inches wide, unblocked

Yarn
Version 1 (page 74):
Cascade Yarns 128 Superwash [100% superwash merino Wool; 128 yd/117 m per 3.5 oz/100 g skein]; color: 1960; 4 skeins

Version 2 (page 77):
Blue Moon Fiber Arts De-Vine [100% superwash merino wool; 225 yd per 8 oz skein]; color: Jasper; 2 skeins

Needles
US #10.5 [6.5 mm] needles, or size appropriate to yarn

Either double-pointed needles or circular needles can be used

Notions
Stitch marker
Waste yarn

Gauge
12 st/20 rows = 4 inches St st, unblocked

Substitutions
Any worsted-, Aran-, or bulky-weight yarn that feels good around your neck. Worsted- and Aran-weight yarns will make a smaller scarf.

Toe-Up Stitch Pattern

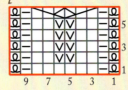

Rnd 1: *K1-tbl, p1, k6, p1, k1-tbl, rep from * to end of rnd.
Rnds 2–5: *K1-tbl, p1, k2, sl 2 wyib, k2, p1, k1-tbl, rep from * to end of rnd.
Rnd 6: * K1-tbl, p1, RDC, LDC, p1, k1-tbl, rep from * to end of rnd.

Top-Down Stitch Pattern

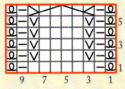

Rnd 1: *K1-tbl, p1, k6, p1, k1-tbl, rep from * to end of rnd.
Rnds 2–5: * K1-tbl, p1, sl 1 wyib, k4, sl 1 wyib, p1, k1-tbl, rep from * to end of rnd.
Rnd 6: * K1-tbl, p1, LDC, RDC, p1, k1-tbl, rep from * to end of rnd.

- ☐ Knit
- ☒ Ktbl
- ⊟ Purl
- ☐ Pattern repeat
- ☑ Sl 1 purlwise with yarn held to WS
- ◩ RDC (Right dropped cable)
- ◪ LDC (Left dropped cable)

Pattern Notes
You may either knit two top-down socks, or two toe-up socks, or one of each from toe to toe.

Blocking is not required but will help "open up" the stitch pattern.

If you secure the ends of your yarn as you go along, there's no need to weave them in at the end. The scarf is a closed tube. The ends will not be seen once they are tucked inside.

RDC (right dropped cable): Sl 2; drop next st to front; return sl sts to LH needle; return dropped st to LH needle (sts have changed places); k3.

LDC (left dropped cable): Drop next st to front; k2; return dropped st to LH needle; k1.

Instructions
First decide if you want to make two toe-up socks, two top-down socks, or one of each.

To make one sock toe-up and one sock top-down:
Complete the instructions for a toe-up sock. At the top of the ribbing, purl one round.

Continue, working the instructions for a top-down sock.

To make two toe-up socks:
Complete the instructions for a toe-up sock. Do not bind off.

Break yarn and complete a second toe-up sock. Do not bind off.
With wrong sides together, use a 3-needle BO to join the two socks.

To make two top-down socks:
Working on Needle 1 only, complete the instructions for a top-down sock.

After completing the first sock, break the yarn and refasten it to work the held sts on Needle 2. Purl 1 rnd.

Continue, working the instructions for a second top-down sock.

Toe-Up Sock
Using Judy's Magic Cast-On, CO 6 st to each needle—12 st total.

Toe
Rnd 1: Place BOR marker (instep side), k6, pm (sole side), k6.
Rnd 2: K1, KLL, k to 1 st before end of instep side, KRL, k2 slipping marker, KLL, k to one st before end of rnd, KRL, k1.

Rep [Rnds 1 and 2], slipping markers when you come to them, until there are 40 sts total.

Foot
Following either the chart or the written instructions for the Toe-Up Stitch Pattern (both on page 76), begin working Toe-Up Stitch Pattern across instep side of foot. K the sts on the sole side of the foot. Rep the Toe-Up Stitch Pattern 3 times.

Gusset
Rnd 1: Instep side: Work in est patt,
  Sole side: K1-tbl, KLL, k to one st before end of rnd, KRL, k1-tbl.
Rnd 2: Instep side: Work in est patt,
  Sole side: K1-tbl, p1, k to 2 st before end of rnd, p1, k1-tbl.

Rep [Rnds 1 and 2] 8 more times, ending with Rnd 6 of Toe-Up Stitch Pattern—20 st on instep side, 38 st on sole side, 58 st total.

Heel turn
Row 1: K1-tbl, p1, k12, KLL, k10, KRL, turn—40 heel sts.
Row 2: Sl 1, p9, turn.
Row 3: KLL, k8, KRL, turn—42 heel sts.
Row 4: Sl 1, p7, turn.
Row 5: KLL, k3, KRL, k3, KRL, k3, ssk, turn—44 heel sts.
Row 6: Sl 1, p15, p2tog, turn—43 heel sts.
Row 7: [Sl 1, k1] eight times, ssk, turn—42 heel sts.
Row 8: Sl 1, p15, p2tog, turn—41 heel sts.
Rep [Rows 7 and 8] until 23 heel sts remain, ending with Row 8.

Last Row: Sl 1, k6, k2tog, k7, ssk, k2, do not turn—21 heel sts.
Go back to working in the round.

Swept Off My Feet

Swept Off My Feet, Version 2

Leg
Rnd 1: Instep side: Work Rnd 1 of Toe-Up Stitch Pattern;
  Sole side: K1-tbl, p1, drop next st behind work, k1, replace dropped st on LH needle, k2tog, k4, p1, k2-tbl, p1, k6, p1, k1-tbl—20 heel sts, 40 sts total.
Rnd 2: Work next rnd of Toe-Up Stitch Pattern, rep 4 times total, to end of rnd.

Continue working in established pattern around leg until the Toe-Up Stitch Pattern has been worked 14 times on the leg.

Swept Off My Feet

Ribbing
Rib pattern: * [K1, p1] twice, k1; rep from * to end of rnd.
Work ribbing for 3 inches.

Top-Down Sock
Using JMCO, CO 20 sts to each needle—40 stitches total. Join to work in the round.

Leg
Rib pattern: * [K1, p1] twice, k1; rep from * to end of rnd.
Work ribbing for 3 inches

Begin working Top-Down Stitch Pattern around leg. Rep until the Top-Down Stitch Pattern has been worked 14 times.

Last rnd: [K1-tbl, p1, k6, p1, k1-tbl] twice. Do not complete rnd. The heel will be worked over the remaining sts of the rnd.

Heel Flap
Row 1: K1-tbl, p1, k8, m1, k8, turn—21 heel sts.
Row 2: Sl 1, p16, turn.
Row 3: [Sl 1, k1] 8 times, k1, turn.

Rep [Rows 2 and 3] 9 more times.
Rep [Row 2] once more.

Heel Turn
Row 1: Sl 1, k6, k2tog, k2, ssk, k1, turn.
Row 2: Sl 1, p5, p2tog, p1 turn.
Row 3: Sl 1, k6, ssk, k1, turn.
Row 4: Sl 1, p7, p2tog, p1, turn.
Row 5: Sl 1, k8, ssk, turn.
Row 6: Sl 1, p8, p2tog, turn.
Row 7: K10 across top of heel flap, pick up and knit 12 sts along side of heel flap, p1, k1-tbl. Do not turn.

Gusset
Note: the Top-Down Stitch Pattern, starting with Rnd 2, will be worked across the instep side of the foot. Rnd 1 of the Stitch Pattern was worked before the heel turn.
Rnd 1: (Rnd 2 of Top-Down Stitch Pattern) [k1-tbl, p1, sl 1 wyib, k4, sl 1 wyib, p1, k1-tbl] twice, k1-tbl, p1, pick up and knit 12 sts along side of heel flap, k to end of rnd.
Rnd 2: Instep side: Work next rnd of Top-Down Stitch Pattern,
Sole side: K1-tbl, p2tog, k to 3 sts before end of rnd, p2tog, k1-tbl.
Rnd 3: Instep side: Work next rnd of Top-Down Stitch Pattern,
Sole side: K1-tbl, p1, k to 2 sts before end of rnd, p1, k1-tbl.

Repeat [Rnds 2 and 3] until 20 sts remain on sole side—40 sts total.
Work in est patt until Top-Down Stitch Pattern has been rep 3 more times, ending with Rnd 1.

Toe
Rnd 1: Ssk, k to 2 sts from end of instep side, k2tog, ssk, knit to last 2 sts, k2tog.
Rnd 2: K around.
Repeat [Rnds 1 and 2] until 12 sts total remain.
Using Kitchener stitch, graft end closed.

Finishing
Pull any loose ends to the inside of the tube. Block if desired.

Swept Off My Feet, Version 1

Mittens

80

Bobsled Mittens

Not only are these mittens shaped like bobsleds, you'll also feel like you are riding the track as you knit your way around the turns.

This pattern doesn't begin to resemble a mitten until you get quite far along in the knitting, so it requires a measure of knitting faith. It starts with JMCO, is knit entirely in the round using the magic loop method, and requires no seaming or picking up of stitches. The multiple directions of the stitches creates a mitten that hugs your hand for a sporty, comfortable fit. Bobsled mittens can be made for many different-sized hands using one set of instructions in various stitch gauges.

Lorilee Beltman

Bobsled Mittens

Sizes
Child's medium (Child's large/Woman's small, Woman's medium, Woman's large/Man's medium, Man's large)

Finished Measurements
Circumference at palm: 7 (8, 8.5, 9, 9.5) inches

Yarn

Version 1 (page 80):
Cascade 220 Tweed [100% wool, 220 yd/202 m per 100g skein]; color: #7607; 1 skein

Version 2 (page 82):
Knit One, Crochet Too Ty-Dy Wool [100% wool; 218 yd/200 m per 100 g skein]; color: Tropicale; #3767; 1 skein

Version 3 (page 84):
Rowan Colourscape Chunky [100% lambswool; 175 yd/160 m per 100 g skein]; color: Bracken; #441; 1 skein

Version 4 (page 85):
Cascade Eco Duo [70% undyed baby alpaca, 30% undyed merino wool; 197 yd m per 100 g skein]; color: #1702; 2 skeins

Needles

Child medium
1 US #5 [3.75 mm] 40-inch circular needle, or size needed to obtain gauge

Child large/Woman's small:
1 US #6 [4.0 mm] 40-inch circular needle, or size needed to obtain gauge

Woman's medium:
1 US #7 [4.5 mm] 40-inch circular needle, or size needed to obtain gauge

Woman's large/Man's medium; Felted Woman's medium
1 US #8 [5.0 mm] 40-inch circular needle, or size needed to obtain gauge

Man's large:
1 US #9 [5.5 mm] 40-inch circular needle, or size needed to obtain gauge

Notions
Two 12-inch lengths of smooth waste yarn in a contrasting color. Tapestry needle.

Gauge
Pattern sizing is dependent upon gauge. Select the gauge which corresponds to selected size.

22 (18, 16, 15, 14) st = 4 inches in St st

Gauges in between these listed will yield mittens in between sizes.

Substitutions
Since this is a proportional design dependent on stitch gauge, many yarns and combinations of yarns can be used for substitutions. Self-striping yarns yield a bold, graphic result.

Pattern Notes
These are intended to be close-fitting mittens. For best fit, select the finished size equal to actual palm circumference.

For felted sizes, select one size up from desired finished size, then shrink to fit following finishing instructions. The proportions remain intact through the felting process. Felted versions must be made from a fiber that will felt.

Bobsled Schematic

- - - - Cast-On
✕✕✕✕ Centered Double Decrease Line
→ Direction of Work

Bobsled Mittens, Version 2

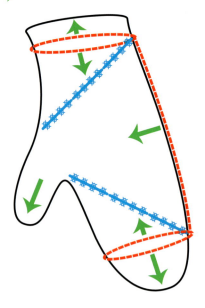

Bobsled Mittens

Refer to Bobsled Schematic on page 82. The cast-on edge (red dashed line) includes some stitches that will be placed on holders, and some stitches that will be worked to form the center palm section. The held stitches will later be worked to form the top and cuff. The center is worked in alternating regular and decrease rounds and ends with the thumb. The arrows indicate the direction in which the work builds.

Instructions
Make two alike.

Cast On
With both ends of 40-inch circular needle held together (see materials list for sizes), hold a tail 7 (8, 8, 9, 9) feet long over the forefinger.

With the bottom needle getting the first stitch, use JMCO to cast on 94 sts on the bottom needle and 93 sts on the top needle—187 sts total. Trim tail to 8 inches.

Set-up Round
Point both needle tips to the right, as to begin knitting a first round.

Orient needle with first-in-line st on top. The ridge of purl bumps from the cast-on is at the back of work.

Extract bottom needle tip out and toward the right for access to top-needle sts.

Set-up Diagram

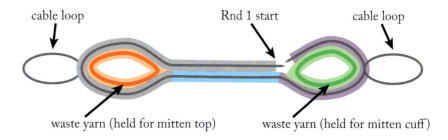

- first 32 stitches from Needle 1 on waste yarn
- second 31 stitches from Needle 1 knit
- last 31 stitches from Needle 1 on waste yarn
- first 31 stitches from Needle 2 knit
- stitches not worked during set-up (first 62 stitches of Rnd 1)

Thread a 12-inch piece of smooth, contrasting colored waste yarn onto a tapestry needle. Transfer the first 32 sts from top needle onto waste yarn. Gather waste yarn tips with cast-on tail and tie securely together, leaving a ring of held sts large enough to fit four fingers.

Pick up bottom needle tip and working yarn, extract needle's cable loop from about halfway point of the held sts to enable Magic Loop knitting. Join, being careful not to twist, and knit next 31 sts from the top needle.

Keep careful count. Markers are neither needed nor recommended yet; just count carefully. After knitting 31 sts, count ahead to check your work; there should be 31 unworked sts remaining on the LH needle.

Thread another 12-inch piece of waste yarn onto a tapestry needle and transfer the remaining 31 sts from the LH needle onto the waste yarn. Tie ends together securely, leaving a ring of held sts large enough to fit four fingers.

Extract cable loop from about halfway point of the second set of held sts to enable Magic Loop knitting with the LH needle again. Join, being careful not to twist, and knit the next 31 sts. (Note: these sts are on Needle 2 and begin the second side of the set-up round.)

This ends the set-up round. Your work should resemble the set-up diagram shown above.

Bobsled Mittens

Center Palm/Back Section

Rnd 1: Ssk, pm on that st (not on the cable), k28, CDD, k14 {loop} k14, CDD, k28, CDD, k15 {loop} k14 to marked st—117 sts total, excluding sts on holders.

Rnd 2: Knit to 1 st before marked st, keeping {loops} positioned as est.

*Bobsled Mittens, Version 3
Also shown: Haberdasher, page 30*

Rnd 3: CDD (uses the final st of Rnd 2 with first 2 sts of Rnd 3, centered over the ssk from previous rnd below), k26, CDD, k13 {loop} k13, CDD, k26, CDD, k14 {loop} k13 to end of round—109 stitches total.

Rnd 4: Rep Rnd 2

Rnd 5: CDD, k24, CDD, k12 {loop} k12, CDD, k24, CDD, k13 {loop} k12 to end of rnd—101 sts total.

Rnd 6: Rep Rnd 2

Rnds 7 – 22: Continue in this manner, alternating dec rnds and knit rnds, and keeping CDD's in line—37 sts.

Rnd 23: CDD, k6, CDD, k3 {loop} k3, CDD, k6, CDD, k4 {loop} k3—29 sts.

Rnd 24: K to last 3 sts of rnd. Place new BOR marker on needle here at the {loop}, which is 3 sts before CDD st from the prior rnd.

Thumb Shaping

Rnd 1: K2, k2tog, k5, CDD, k2 {loop} k2, CDD, k5, ssk, k3 {loop}—23 sts.

Rnd 2: K11 {loop} k8, k1-tbl, k3 {loop}

Rnd 3: K1, k2tog, k5, ssk, k1 {loop} k1, k2tog, k5, ssk, k2 {loop}—19 sts.

Rnd 4: K7, k1-tbl, k1 {loop} k7, k1-tbl, k2 {loop}.

Rnd 5: K2tog, k7, KLL {loop} KRL, k7, ssk, k1 {loop}.

Rnd 6: K9 {loop} k8 to last 2 sts of rnd {reposition loop here}. Remove BOR marker.

Shuffle these last 2 sts ahead to next needle. Place BOR marker.

Rnd 7: CDD, k8, KLL {loop} KRL, k8 {loop}

Rnd 8: K10 {loop} k8 to last st of rnd {loop}. Shuffle the last st ahead to next needle. Mark new BOR.

Rep [Rnds 7 and 8] 4 (4, 4, 4, 5) more times, or until thumb measures 1/2-inch short of desired length, ending having completed a Rnd 8—19 sts.

Final Thumb Tip Shaping

CDD, k7 {loop} ssk, k6 {loop} CDD, k5 {loop} CDD, k4 {loop} CDD, k3 {loop} CDD, k2 {loop}, CDD, k1 {loop} CDD, k1.

Break yarn. Thread tail through rem 4 sts and remove the sts from the needle. Pull the opening closed and darn tail to inside.

Mitten Top

Insert circular needle into sts held on waste yarn at mitten top. Rem waste yarn.

Although this is the section that initially had 32 sts when the waste yarn was inserted, it is common for a st to get lost in this process, leaving 31 sts.

Note: be certain there are 32 sts before beginning Rnd 1, picking up and knitting a st if necessary.

Bobsled Mittens

Join new yarn at point where diagonal lines from CDD converge by pinky area of mitten (refer to pattern schematic on page 82). Find the st emerging from the intersection of the diagonal lines and mark it as the first st of the round.

Rnd 1: {Loop} k16 {loop} k16.
Rnd 2: {Loop} k16 {loop} k15 {loop}. Shuffle the last st ahead to next rnd.
Rnd 3: CDD, k14 {loop} k15—30 sts.
Rnd 4: {Loop} k15 {loop} k14 {loop}. Shuffle the last st ahead to next rrd.
Rnd 5: CDD, k13 {loop} k14 to end of rnd—28 sts.
Rnd 6: {Loop} k14 {loop} k13 {loop}. Shuffle the last st ahead to next rnd.
Rnd 7: CDD, k 11 {loop} CDD, k11 {loop}—24 sts.
Rnd 8: K12 {loop} k11 {loop}. Shuffle the last st ahead to next rnd.
Rnd 9: CDD, k9 {loop} CDD, k9 {loop}—20 sts.
Rnd 10: K10 {loop} k9 {loop}. Shuffle the last st ahead to next rnd.
Rnd 11: CDD, k7 {loop} CDD, k7 {loop}—16 sts.
Rnd 12: K8 {loop} k7 {loop}. Shuffle the last st ahead to next rnd.

Next, finish the mitten top. Adjust {loops} as necessary to accomplish the following: CDD, k5, CDD, k4, CDD, k3, CDD, k2, CDD, k1. Break yarn.

Thread tail through rem 6 sts and remove the sts from the needle. Pull the opening closed and darn tail to inside.

Mitten Cuff

Insert circular needle into 31 sts held on waste yarn at mitten cuff. Remove waste yarn.

Join new yarn at point where diagonal lines from CDD's converge (refer to pattern schematic on page 82). Pick up 1 st from intersection of these lines, taking care not to create a hole—32 sts.

Knit 2 rnds.

Bind off in 2-st applied I-cord as follows:

CO 1 st to LH needle. *K1, k2togtbl, replace these 2 sts to LH needle; working loosely, rep from * to end of rnd—2 sts rem on RH needle.

Break yarn and use tail to graft final sts to beg of BO rnd for a smooth, continuous edge.

Bobsled Mittens, Version 4
Also shown: Monica's Seamen's Scarf, page 68

Finishing

Darn tails to inside. Block lightly.

For felted version, soak in hot water with a dash of low-sudsing soap. Wear wet mittens and rub them together vigorously, working all surface areas until shrunk to desired size. Lay flat to dry.

Over The Top Mittens

I've always admired stranded mitten designs with stripes of color that run continuously from the cuff, around the hand, over the thumb, and back to the cuff. One day, the idea popped into my head, "Wouldn't it be fun to have a cable running around the edge of a mitten?"

It took several tries to get the tip of the hand and the tip of the thumb just right, but I'm thrilled with the results.

JC Briar

Over The Top Mittens

Sizes
S (M, L, XL)
Hand circumference: 7 (7.75, 8.25, 9) inches

Yarn
Version 1 (page 86):
Zitron Ecco [100% extrafine merino; 110 m per 50 g skein]; color: 151; 2 (3, 3, 3) skeins
Version 2 (page 89):
Zitron Ecco [100% extrafine merino; 110 m per 50 g skein]; color: 123; 2 (3, 3, 3) skeins

Needles
1 set US #5 [3.75 mm] needles, or size needed to obtain gauge
Either double-pointed or circular needles may be used

Notions
Cable needle
Stitch markers in 3 colors: to indicate beginning of rnds, locations of cables, and locations of gusset decreases
St holders or waste yarn

Gauge
24 sts/38 rows = 4 inches in St st

Substitutions
You can substitute any DK-weight yarn that knits to gauge. Wool yarns will keep your hands the warmest. Plain, smooth yarns will show off the cabling.

This pattern was first published in *Twists and Turns® The Newsletter for Lovers of Cable Knitting*, in the Winter 2009 issue.

Pattern Notes
The hand and thumb are worked separately from the tip down to the "crotch" of the thumb, then joined.

Rope Cable (over 6 sts):
Rnds 1–3: P1, k4, p1.
Rnd 4: P1, c4f, p1.
Repeat [Rnds 1–3] for patt.

C4f (cable 4 front): Slip next two sts to cable needle and hold in front, k2, k2 sts from cable needle

Cdi (Centered Double Increase): [K1-tbl, k1] in next st, insert LH needle from left to right under vertical strand between sts just made, knit this strand

Instructions
Hand
Starting with a 12-inch tail, JMCO 7 sts onto each of two needles—14 sts total.
Pm for BOR.
Work as follows (if using dpns, divide sts onto additional dpns during set-up rnd):

Set-up rnd: Cdi, place cable marker, p1, k4, p1, cdi, place cable marker, p1, c4f, p1—18 sts.
Rnd 1: [Knit to cable marker, work Rope Cable] twice.
Rnd 2: [KRL, knit to cable marker, KLL, slip marker, work Rope Cable] twice—22 sts.

Rep [Rnds 1 and 2] 7 (8, 9, 10) more times—50 (54, 58, 62) sts.

Work even in pattern as est, omitting KRL and KLL increases, until Hand measures 5 (5.75, 6.5, 7) inches or desired length to "crotch" of thumb; end having worked Rnd 4 of Rope Cable. Cut yarn, leaving 12-inch tail. Place sts on hold.

Thumb
Work as for Hand until Thumb has 22 (26, 26, 30) sts.

Work even in pattern as est until Thumb measures 2.5 (2.75, 3, 3.25) inches or desired length to "crotch" of thumb; end having worked Rnd 4 of Rope Cable.

Join Hand and Thumb
K across Thumb sts to first cable marker, place next 6 Thumb sts (Rope Cable sts) on hold.

K first st from Hand, place dec marker, work in patt as est to last 7 Hand sts, place dec marker, k1, place last 6 Hand sts (Rope Cable sts) on holder or waste yarn.

Work in patt as est to end of Thumb sts—60 (68, 72, 80) sts.
Rnds now begin after Rope Cable at edge of Thumb.

Over The Top Mittens

Thumb Gusset

Continuing with Rope Cable patt as est, dec 2 sts every 3 rnds 5 (7, 7, 9) times as follows: work to 2 sts before first dec marker, k2tog, work to second dec marker, ssk, work to end of rnd—50 (54, 58, 62) sts. Remove dec markers and work even in patt as est until mitten measures 7.5 (8.25, 9, 9.75) inches or desired length to start of cuff.

Cuff

Next rnd: dec and est rib pattern as follows:

Sizes S and L: [K1, ssk, *p1, k2tog, k1, rep from * to cable marker, work Rope Cable as est] twice—40 (46) sts rem.

Sizes M and XL: [K2, *p1, k2tog, k1, rep from * to 3 sts before cable marker, p1, k2, work Rope Cable as est] twice—46 (52) sts rem.

Work even in k2, p1 rib and Rope Cable as est until cuff measures 2.5 (2.75, 2.75, 3) inches or desired length; end having worked Rnd 4 of Rope Cable.
Bind off loosely in pattern.

Finishing

Using yarn tail attached to Hand, graft juncture between Hand and Thumb closed, or turn mitten inside-out and close juncture with 3-needle BO.

Darn in ends. Wash and block according to yarn manufacturer's instructions.

Over The Top Mittens, Version 2

Over The Top Mittens

Over The Top Mittens, Version 1

Socks

92

Spring Fever Socks

When the seasons come around to spring, I am always entranced by the shiny newness of the first green budding of leaves in my garden. These socks start from Judy's Magic Cast-On toes and open up into a delightful leafy pattern. The delicate leaf columns of the Spring Fever socks are not only decorative, they also function as a widely spaced ribbing providing compression and elasticity. Because the socks are made from the toe up it's easy to make them as long or short as you like.

Janel Laidman

Spring Fever Socks

Sizes
Women's Small (Medium, Large)

Finished Measurements
Circumference unstretched
7.8 inches (8.25 inches, 9 inches)

Yarn
Version 1 (page 93):
Abstract Fibers Supersock [100% superwash merino wool; 382 yd per 3.5 oz skein]; color: Gold; 1 skein

Version 2 (page 95):
Malabrigo Sock [100% pure superwash merino wool; 440 yd per 3.5 oz skein]; color: Impressionist Sky; 1 skein

Needles
US #1 [2.5 mm] circular or double-pointed needles or size needed to obtain gauge

Notions
Tapestry needle

Gauge
8 sts/11 rows = 1 inch in St st knit in the round

Substitutions
Fingering or sock-weight yarn in solid or semi-solid colors

Pattern Notes
Length of foot is measured by trying on sock. This pattern has 3 sizes in circumference; you may also change sizes by changing needle and yarn size.

Instructions
Using Judy's Magic Cast-On, CO 13 sts to each of two needles—26 sts total.

Sts are divided into two groups: 13 instep sts and 13 sole sts.

Toe
Rnd 1: Knit.
Rnd 2: Instep sts: K1, M1, k to last st, M1, k1;
Sole sts: Work as for instep sts—30 sts.

Rep [Rnds 1 and 2] 8 (9, 10) times—62 (66, 72) sts.

Stop increasing and finish rnd even as soon as the desired number is reached.

Foot
Redistribute sts as follows: 31 (33, 37) instep sts and 31 (33, 36) sole sts.

Begin Chart 1
Rnd 1: Instep sts: Beginning and ending as indicated on the chart for the size you are working, work Chart 1;
Sole sts: Knit.

When Chart 1 is complete, begin Chart 2.
Cont Sole sts in St st and work Instep sts following Chart 2 as follows:
Size small: P2, [work Charted Sts 2-10] 3 times, p2.
Size medium: [Work Charted Sts 1-11] 3 times.
Size large: Beginning at St 6 of Chart 2, work Sts 6-10, then [Sts 2-10] 3 times, then Sts 2-6 (3 full motifs, and 2 half-motifs).

Continue to work foot in this manner until it measures approximately 3 inches less than overall foot length.

Gusset
Rnd 1: Instep sts: Continue following Chart 2 as est.
Sole sts: K1, M1, k to last st, M1, k1—33 (35, 37) heel sts.
Rnd 2: Work even, continuing patt as est.

Rep [Rnds 1 and 2} until you have 49 (51, 53) sole sts; end having completed the instep sts.

Heel Turn
Row 1 (RS): K 16, place marker 1, k16 (18, 20), M1, wrap next st, pm 2, turn—16

Spring Fever Socks

sts at each side and 18 (20, 22) sts between markers.

Row 2: P16 (18, 20), M1p, w&t.
Row 3: K15 (17, 19), M1, w&t.
Row 4: P14 (16, 18) M1p, w&t.
Row 5: K13 (15, 17), M1, w&t.
Row 6: P12 (14, 16), M1p, w&t.
Row 7: K11 (13, 15), M1, w&t.
Row 8: P10 (12, 14), M1p, w&t.
Row 9: K9 (11, 13), M1, w&t.
Row 10: P8 (10, 12), M1p, w&t.
Row 11: K7 (9, 11), M1, w&t.
Row 12: P6 (8, 10), M1, w&t.
Row 10: K5 (7, 9), M1, w&t.
Row 11: P4 (6, 8), M1. Do not turn—31 (33, 35) sts between markers.

Continuing across the row, purl to 1 st before Marker 1, picking up wraps and purling tog with the sts that they wrap; removing Marker 1, purl next 2 sts tog, turn.

Row 12: Sl 1, knit to 1 st before Marker 2, picking up rem wraps and knitting with the sts that they wrap; removing Marker 2, ssk, turn.

Pick Up Flap

Row 1 (WS): Sl 1, k1 (5, 7), *p1 tbl, k8 (10, 8); rep from * twice (once, once) more. P1 tbl, k1 (5, 7), ssk, turn.
Row 2: Sl 1, p1 (5, 7), *k1-tbl, p8 (10, 8); rep from * twice (once, once) more. K1-tbl, p1 (5, 7) p2 tog, turn.

Rep [Rows 1 and 2] until 31 (33, 35) heel sts rem and all side heel sts have been incorporated, ending with a Row 1.

Next row (RS): Sl 1, work in patt as est to end of heel sts.

Cuff

Rnd 1: Instep sts: Work in patt as est;
Heel sts: Continue in patt as already est on the Instep sts to end of rnd.

Continue in this manner until cuff measures approximately 6 inches and you have completed a leaf portion of the chart.

Ribbing

Size small and large only: *K1-tbl, P2, repeat from * to end of rnd.
Size medium only: Follow Chart 3 (medium).

Rep ribbing for 9 rnds.

Bind Off

Use Elizabeth Zimmermann's sewn bind-off or other stretchy bind-off.

Spring Fever Socks, version 2

Spring Fever Socks

Chart 1 (medium)

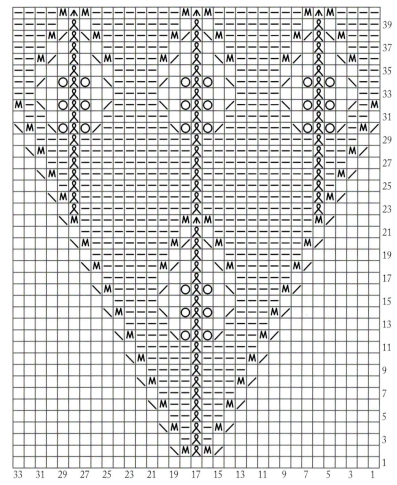

Chart 2

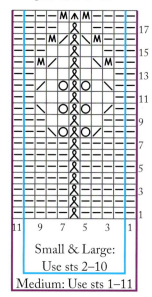

Small & Large: Use sts 2–10
Medium: Use sts 1–11

- ☐ Knit
- ⊟ Purl on RS, knit on WS
- ╱ K2tog
- ╲ SSK
- ⏀ Ktbl on RS, ptbl on WS
- ⋀ CDD (centered double decrease)
- ◯ Yarn over
- M M1P by lifting bar between stitches and purling tbl
- M For size L: M1P
  For size S: purl

Chart 3

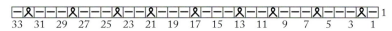

Spring Fever Socks

Chart 1 (small and large)

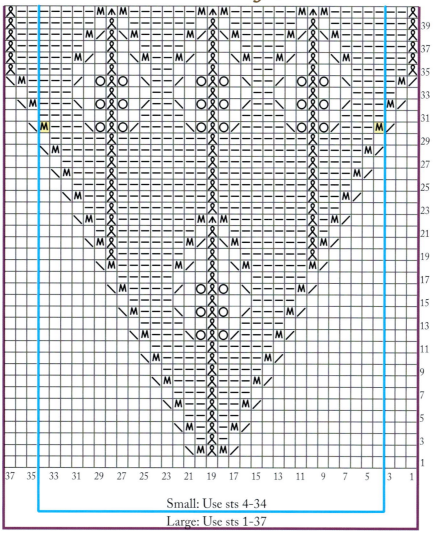

Small: Use sts 4-34
Large: Use sts 1-37

Socks Beyond Toes

Three-Point Socks

Shortly after I learned to knit socks with afterthought heels, I noticed that the fabric tended to pull tight across the instep, and bulge a little at the back of the heel. This sock addresses both issues by using a herringbone fabric. Because herringbone fabric slants diagonally in alternate directions, you can orient the 3 "points" of the leg, heel, and cuff towards the ankle. This gives some ease to the instep, and at the same time, pulls the heel up in the back so it doesn't bulge. Visually, the joining of the 3 points creates an interesting-looking ankle from the side, and the 10-stitch panel in the front provides a canvas for lace or other decorative pattern.

Jeny Staiman

Three-Point Socks

Finished Measurements
Circumference unstretched: 8 inches
Will stretch to fit up to 9 inches on the foot and 10 inches on the leg

Yarn
Version 1 (page 98, right):
Blue Moon Socks That Rock Medium [100% superwash merino wool; 380 yd/347 m per 5.5 oz/155 g skein]; color: Blue Brick Wall; 1 skein

Version 2 (page 98, left):
Pico Accuardi Dyeworks Acid & Weed [100% superwash wool; 380 yd per 3.5 oz/100 g skein]; color: Wicked Freak (one of a kind); 1 skein

Version 3 (with lace, page 102):
Blue Moon Socks That Rock Medium [100% superwash merino wool; 380 yd/347 m per 5.5 oz / 155 g skein]; color: Mossay; 1 skein

Version 4 (with lace, page 103):
Malabrigo Sock [100% superwash merino wool; 440 yd per 3.5 oz skein]; color: Turner; 1 skein

Needles
2 US #2 [2.75 mm] 36-inch (or longer) circular needles, or size needed to obtain gauge

Notions
Stitch markers (optional)
Tapestry needle

Gauge
30 sts/40 rows = 4 inches in St st

Substitutions
Any fingering or sock-weight yarn.

Pattern Notes

This sock is a cousin of the classic afterthought heel sock, but instead of unpicking a row of stitches for the heel, you'll knit the heel first; then cast on a bridge of stitches from one end to the other; and finally work in opposite directions to the cuff and toe.

The Magic Loop method is highly recommended for working the Magic Bridge technique. The remainder of the sock can be worked using one or two circular needles or double-pointed needles.

This pattern uses two separate strands of your main color yarn. You can either use both ends of a center pull ball, or wind into two separate balls. If you use one ball, start with the center pull strand. You can also substitute a length of waste yarn in the Magic Bridge, but you will then need to remove the waste yarn and pick up the live stitches later in the pattern.

Herringbone Pattern (28 sts)
Rnd 1–2: Knit.
Rnd 3: Ssk, k7, KRL, k10, KLL, k7, k2tog.

Rep Rnds 1–3 for patt.

Instructions
Using Judy's Magic Cast-On, CO 12 sts to each needle—24 stitches total.

Heel
Heel shaping rows, worked on 1 needle only:
Row 1 (RS): K10, w&t.
Row 2 (WS): P8, w&t.
Row 3: K7, w&t.
Row 4: P6, w&t.
Row 5: K9, concealing the wraps as you come to them.
After the set-up rows, turn to the other needle and begin working in the round.
Rnd 1: Needle 1: K2, KLL, k1, KRL, k6, KLL, k1, KRL, k2.
Needle 2: K1, KLL, k2 concealing wraps, KRL, k6, KLL, k2, KRL, k1—16 sts each side, 32 sts total.
Rnd 2: Knit.
Rnd 3: Needle 1: K2, KLL, k3, KRL, k6, KLL, k3, KRL, k2.
Needle 2: K1, KLL, k4, KRL, k6, KLL, k4, KRL, k1—20 sts each side, 40 sts total.
Rnds 4–5: Knit.
Rnd 6: Needle 1: K2, KLL, k to 2 st from end, KRL, k2.
Needle 2: K1, KLL, k to last st, KRL, k1—22 sts each side, 44 sts total.

Three-Point Socks

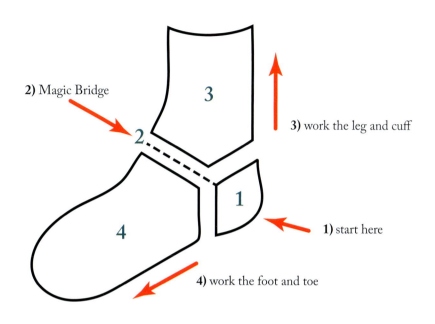

Rnds 7–15: Rep [Rnds 4–6] 3 times—28 sts each side, 56 sts total.
Rnd 16: Knit.
Rnd 17: Needle 1: Sl 1, k to last st, sl 1. Stop; do not work Needle 2.

Instep

Following steps 1–5 of "Adding Stitches With JMCO—Magic Bridge" on page 20, using the working yarn and the tail from a second strand of yarn, CO 40 sts to each needle—80 sts total.

Each needle now holds 68 sts: 28 original heel sts, and 40 new instep sts.

Pull a loop of cable from between the heel and instep sts to begin working in the rnd using the Magic Loop method.

Instep to Leg

Note: Begin working Herringbone Pattern on 28 sts of Heel Side.

Rnds 1–2: Knit.
Rnd 3: Heel side: Work Rnd 3 of Herringbone Pattern.
   (Instep side): Ssk, k to 2 st from end, k2tog—28 heel sts and 38 instep sts; 66 sts total.
Rnd 4–9: Rep [Rnds 1–3] twice more—28 heel sts and 34 instep sts; 60 sts total.
Rnd 10–11: Knit.

Leg

The front of the sock may be left plain, or a lace pattern may be inserted in the center.

To insert the lace pattern, replace the Instep Side instructions for Rnds 1–9 with Chart A. Then, beginning with Rnd 10, replace the Instep Side instructions for the remaining rnds with Chart B. Rep Chart B as necessary for the length of the leg.

The lace pattern may also be worked on the back of the leg by replacing both the Heel Side and Instep Side instructions with Chart B beginning with Rnd 10.

Rnd 1: (Heel side): Ssk, k7, KRL, k10, KLL, k7, k2tog.
   (Instep side): Ssk, k11, yo, ssk, k4, k2tog, yo, k11, k2tog.

Rnd 2–3: K around.
Rnd 4: (Heel side): Ssk, k7, KRL, k10, KLL, k7, k2tog.
   (Instep side): Ssk, k11, yo, ssk, k2, k2tog, yo, k11, k2tog.
Rnd 5–6: K around.
Rnd 7: (Heel side): Ssk, k7, KRL, k10, KLL, k7, k2tog.
   (Instep side): Ssk, k11, yo, ssk, k2tog, yo, k11, k2tog—28 sts on each needle, 56 sts total.
Rnds 8–9: Knit.

If desired, begin Chart B with next rnd.

Three-Point Socks

Three-Point Socks, version 3

Rnd 1: (Heel side): Pick up 1 st in the gap between the instep and the heel, k to end of heel side, pick up 1 st in the gap between the heel and the instep.
(Instep side): K around—40 instep sts and 30 heel sts, 70 sts total.

Rnd 2: (Heel side): Sl 1 pwise, k to last st, sl 1 pwise.
(Instep side): Knit.

Rnd 3: Knit.

Rnd 4: [Ssk, knit to last 2 sts, k2tog] twice—38 instep sts and 28 heel sts, 66 sts total.

Rnd 5–6: Knit.

Rnd 7: (Heel side): Ssk, k7, KRL, k10, KLL, k7, k2tog. (36 instep sts and 28 heel sts, 64 sts total)
(Instep side): Ssk, knit to 2 from end, k2tog.

Rnd 8–13: Rep [Rnds 5–7] twice more—32 instep sts and 28 heel sts, 60 sts total.

Rnd 14–15: Knit.

Rnd 10: [Ssk, k7, KRL, k10, KLL, k7, k2tog] 2 times.
Rnds 11–12: Knit.
Repeat [Rnds 10–12] 10 more times.

Cuff

Rnds 1–8: *K1, p1; rep from * around.

If desired, work additional rounds of ribbing for a longer cuff.

BO the cuff using Jeny's Surprisingly Stretch Bind-Off or other stretchy bind-off.

Instep to Foot

Start from instep and work to the toe. If necessary, slide the sts along the needle until you come to the working yarn (see Step 7 of "Adding Stitches With JMCO—Magic Bridge" on page 21).

Pull a loop of cable from between the heel and instep sts to begin working in the round using the Magic Loop method. There will be 28 sts on the heel side, and 40 sts on the instep side.

Three-Point Socks

Foot

The top of the foot may be left plain, or the lace pattern may be inserted in the center. Chart A and Chart B can be found on page 104.

To insert the lace pattern, replace the Instep side instructions for Rnds 1–9 with Chart A. Then, beginning with Rnd 10, replace the instep side instructions for the remaining rnds with Chart B, repeating Chart B as necessary for the length of the foot.

Rnd 1: (Heel side): Ssk, k7, KRL, k10, KLL, k7, k2tog.
  (Instep side): Ssk, k11, ssk, k4, k2tog, k11, k2tog.
Rnd 2–3: Knit.
Rnd 4: (Heel side): Ssk, k7, KRL, k10, KLL, k7, k2tog.
  (Instep side): Ssk, k11, ssk, k2, k2tog, k11, k2tog—28 sts on each needle, 56 sts total.
Rnd 5–6: Knit.
Rnd 7: [Ssk, k7, KRL, k10, KLL, k7, k2tog] 2 times.
Rnds 8–9: Knit.

If desired, begin Chart B with next rnd.

Rep [Rnds 7–9] until the sock foot is 2 inches shorter than the desired finished length.

Toe

Rnds 1: Knit.
Rnd 2: [Ssk, k last 2 sts on needle, k2tog] twice—26 sts on each needle, 52 sts total.
Rnds 3–4: Knit.
Rnd 5: [Ssk, k to last 2 sts on needle, k2tog] twice—24 sts on each needle, 48 sts total.
Rnd 6: Knit.
Rnds 7–14: Rep [Rnds 5–6] 4 more times—16 sts on each needle, 32 sts total.
Rnd 15–16: Rep [Rnd 2] twice—12 sts on each needle, 24 sts total.

Toe tip

Setup: K across the heel side. Turn to the instep side. Work the following rows across the Instep Side only:
Row 1 (RS): K10, w&t.
Row 2 (WS): P8, w&t.
Row 3: K7, w&t.
Row 4: P6, w&t.
Row 5: K9, concealing the wraps as you come to them.

Finishing

Graft 24 remaining toe sts closed with Kitchener stitch. Weave in ends.

Three-Point Socks, version 4; also shown: Spring Fever Socks, page 93

Three-Point Socks

Chart A

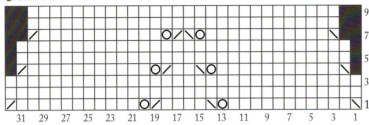

Chart B

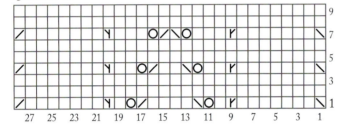

	Knit
╱	K2tog
╲	SSK
O	Yo
ʏ	M1t (make one towards)
ʏ	M1a (make one away)
■	No stitch

Back: Three-Point Socks, Version 1
Front: Three-Point Socks, Version 2

Garments & Wraps

105

Djinn

I love vests! They look great on everyone. They give you just the right amount of indoor warmth and can be mixed and matched with shirts, pants or skirts for oodles of options. Best of all, the smaller canvas encourages me to try out techniques and looks I might be afraid of on a larger scale. Less yarn, less time and more choices—what more could you ask for?

This particular vest's curvy pattern and shape reminded me of a magic lamp and working all those slip-stitches and ending up with a colorful pattern always feels like a bit of magic. Djinn are said to be able to change their shape, to not always be what they seem to be, and to have mysterious magical abilities. I figured that sounded like a description for a great vest.

Samantha Roshak

Djinn

Sizes
Women's XS (S, M, L, 1X)

Vest has zero ease. Make a size up for a looser fit.

Finished Measurements
Chest: 29 (33, 38, 42, 46.5) inches

Length: 22.5 (22.5, 23, 23.5, 24) inches

Yarn
Blue Moon Fiber Arts BFL [100% Blue Faced Leicester wool; 661 yd/604 m per 226 g skein]

Version 1 (shown in size M, page 106, left):

[MC] Manly Yes, but I Like It Too; 1 (1, 1, 1, 2) skein(s)

[CC] My Little Color Brain; 1 (1, 1, 1, 1) skein

Version 2 (shown in size S; page 106, right):

[MC] Meet Brown, Joe; 1 (1, 1, 1, 2) skein(s)

[CC] Blue Brick Wall; 1 (1, 1, 1, 1) skein

Needles
1 US #5 [3.75 mm] circular needle, or size need to obtain gauge

2 US #7 [4.5 mm] circular needles, or size need to obtain gauge

Notions
Tapestry needle

Stitch markers

Stitch holders or waste yarn

Gauge:
18 sts/37 rows = 4 inches in patt (blocked)

20 sts/28 rows = 4 inches in 1x1 ribbing

Substitutions:
Lofty DK-weight wool in contrasting colors. Good choices are Fleece Artist Blue Face Leicester DK, Briar Rose Fibers Legend, or Rowan Pure Wool DK.

Pattern Notes:
This vest is worked with a slip-stitch pattern (also called mosaic knitting), using two colors. Although it looks as if there are two colors per row, you work each row using only one color, with the contrasting color slipped from the row below.

When reading the chart, the column to the right (marked as stitch 0) indicates the active color for that row. Work each stitch in the indicated color and slip all stitches in the other color. Except for the first two setup rows, the color changes every 2 rows.

Carry the yarn not-in-use loosely up the side and behind the last color used.

When working flat, never slip the first or last stitch in the row. Always work those stitches in the active color to make it easier to pick up stitches for the ribbing.

Slip-stitch fabric improves with blocking and gauge can change dramatically. Please wash and block your swatch to insure a good fit and a fabric you are happy with.

To gain the full effects of the pattern choose highly contrasting yarns. Selecting one multi-colored yarn can look great, but be sure that the second yarn you pick has no colors in common with your main color.

This pattern includes waist shaping. The shaping alters the pattern at the sides and can

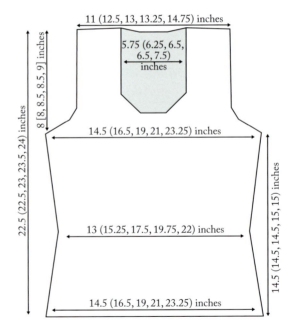

Djinn

be left out, for a straighter or larger fit. If you prefer, follow the pattern to the armhole ignoring all increases and decreases.

Markers are used to designate the "side-seam" stitches—the waist-shaping decreases and increases are made on either side of them. One of these markers is also the beginning of round marker and should be in a different color from the others.

When binding off, weave inactive yarn in along the bind-off so that it's available in the correct position when needed.

1x1 Rib: *K1 ,p1, rep from * to end of rnd.

Instructions

Bottom Ribbing

With larger needles and using JMCO, CO 65 (75, 85, 95, 105) sts to each needle—130 (150, 170, 190, 210) sts total.

Follow instructions for "Invisible Cast-On for Ribbing—Tubular Reef" on page 17 until all the sts are on 1 needle.

Using smaller needle, work 1 rnd 1x1 Rib; pm for BOR and join. (When finishing the vest, you will use the tail to seam the rows you have already worked.)

Cont in rib for 2.5 (2.5, 3, 3, 3) inches. Place markers as follows: Maintaining rib, work 64 (74, 84, 94, 104) sts (front), place Marker 2; work 1 st (side seam), place Marker 3; work to last st, place Marker 4 (back); work last st (side seam).

Begin Body

Rnd 1: Using CC, work Row 1 of Set-up Chart.
Rnd 2: Using MC, work Row 2 of Set-up Chart.
Work 40 rnds following Main Body Chart.

Djinn, Version 2

Garments & Wraps — Beyond Toes

Djinn

Djinn, Version 1

Work all decs and side-seam sts with active color throughout shaping.

Dec for waist shaping [every 8 rnds] 3 times as follows: ssk, work patt to 2 sts before Marker 2, k2tog, sm, k1, sm, ssk, work patt to 2 sts before Marker 4, k2tog, sm, k1. (4 sts dec)

Maintain established pattern for all other rounds—118 (138, 158, 178, 198) sts after all dec.
Work 13 rnds.

Inc for bust shaping [every 8 rnds] 3 times as follows: M1, work est patt to Marker 2, M1, sm, k1, sm, M1, work to Marker 4, M1, sm, k1. (4 sts inc)

Maintain pattern for all other rounds—130 (150, 170, 190, 210) sts after all inc.
Work in est patt until piece measures approximately 14.5 (14.5, 14.5, 15, 15) inches, ending on an even rnd 4 (4, 5, 6, 7) sts short of Marker 4.

Armhole and Neck Shaping

Division Rnd: Removing markers as you come to them, BO 3 (4, 5, 6, 7) sts with the active color; switch colors at the BOR and BO 4 (5, 6, 7, 8) sts; work in est patt to 3 (4, 5, 6, 7) sts before 2nd marker, BO 7 (9, 11, 13, 15), work in est patt to bound off sts—58 (66, 74, 82, 90) sts each front and back.

Front and back are worked separately for the remainder of the vest.

Note: Mark patt row just completed so you will know where to beg when resuming work on the front.

Back Armhole Shaping:

Work all decs and edge sts with active color.

Row 1 (WS): BO 3 (4, 5, 7, 7) sts, work in est patt to end.

Row 2 (RS): BO 3 (4, 5, 7, 7) sts with active color, work in est patt to the end of the row—52 (58, 64, 68, 76) sts.
Row 3: Work even.
Row 4: K1, ssk, work in est patt to last 3 sts, k2tog, k1—50 (56, 62, 66, 74) sts.

Rep last 2 rows 0 (0, 2, 3, 4) more times—50 (56, 58, 60, 66) sts.

Work even until armhole measures approximately 7 (7.5, 8, 8, 8.5) inches, ending on a WS row.

Back Neck Shaping:

Split Sides for Neck (RS): Work 12 (14, 15, 16, 17) sts in est patt for right side of neck; slip center 26 (28, 28, 28, 32) sts to a holder for back neck; hold rem 12 (14, 15, 16, 17) sts for the left side, to be completed after finishing the right side.

Right side:

Work even until armhole depth is 8 (8, 8.5, 8.5, 9) inches. Place sts on a holder. Cut yarn leaving at least a 12-inch tail.

Left side:

Re-join yarn;

Work even until armhole depth is 8 (8, 8.5, 8.5, 9) inches. Place sts on a holder. Cut yarn leaving at least a 12-inch tail.

Djinn

Front Neck and Armhole Shaping:

Work all decs and edge sts with active color.

Row 1 (WS): BO 3 (4, 5, 7, 7) sts, work in est patt to end.

Row 2 (RS): BO 3 (4, 5, 7, 7) sts with active color, work in est patt to the end of the row—52 (58, 64, 68, 76) sts.

Split for Neck Shaping as follows:

Division Row (WS): Work 16 (19, 22, 24, 28) sts in est pat; slip 20 sts to a holder for front neck; hold last 16 (19, 22, 24, 28) sts for the right side.

Left side:

Next row (RS): Dec for armhole and neck 1 (1, 3, 4, 5) times as follows: K1, ssk, work in est patt to the last 3 sts, k2tog, k1—14 (17, 16, 16, 18) sts.

Work remaining neckline decs 2 (3, 1, 0, 1) times as follows: Work in est patt to last 3 sts k2tog, k1—12 (14, 15, 16, 17) sts.

Work even until armhole measures same as for back, ending with a WS row. Put sts on holder.

Right side:

Next row (RS): Dec for armhole and neck 1 (1, 3, 4, 5) times as follows: K1, ssk, work in est patt to the last 3 sts, k2tog, k1—14 (17, 16, 16, 18) sts

Work remaining neckline decs 2 (3, 1, 0, 1) times as follows : K1, ssk, work in est patt to end of row—12 (14, 15, 16, 17) sts.

Work even until armhole measures same as for back, ending with a WS row.

Both Sides:

Use 3-needle BO to join front and back together at the shoulder.

Neck And Armhole Ribbing

Armhole Ribbing:

Starting at the center underarm and using smaller needle and MC, pick up and knit an even number of sts as follows: 3 sts for every 4 rows around the armhole and st-for-st across bound-off sts.

Work 1x1 Rib for 1 inch. BO in patt with larger needle.

Neck Ribbing:

Starting at back neck and using smaller needle and MC, knit across the 18 (26, 28, 28, 32) back neck sts, pick up and knit 3 sts for every 4 rows along the left side of the neck, knit across the 20 front neck sts, pick up and knit 3 sts for every 4 rows along the right side of the neck (adjust as necessary to have an even number); pm for BOR and join.

Work 1x1 Rib for 1 inch. BO in patt with larger needle.

Finishing

Using tail, close short seam at CO edge. Weave in ends.

Wash and block to finished measurements.

Djinn, Version 2
Also shown: November Street, page 120;
Haberdasher, page 30

Djinn

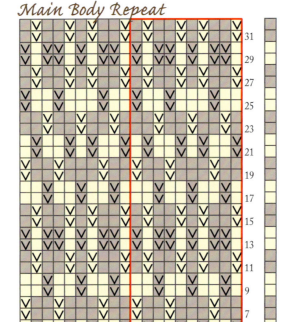

- ☐ With CC: (RS) knit, (WS) purl
- ▨ With MC: (RS) knit, (WS) purl
- ✓ Sl 1 purlwise with yarn held to WS
- ▯ Pattern repeat

Note: The column to the right is the active color for each row.

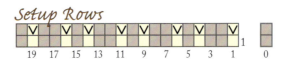

Djinn

Djinn, Version 1
Also shown: Haberdasher, page 30; FlatPack, page 156; Spring Fever Socks, page 92

Pasarela

This casual and comfortable shrug is perfect for those times when a little extra warmth is needed against the cool air. Pasarela is the Spanish word for walkways and the subtle, ribbed pattern of this shrug inspires one to think of long linear paths.

Kathleen Fajardo

Pasarela

Finished Measurements
Chest: 32 (34, 36, 38, 40, 44, 48)
Length: 14 (14.5, 14.5, 15, 15, 16, 16)

Yarn
Stitchjones Superwash Worsted [100% superwash merino wool; 218 yd per 100 g skein]; 3 (3, 4, 4, 5, 5, 6) skeins

Version 1 (shown in size 34-inch chest, page 114):
Color: Sligo

Version 2 (shown in size 36-inch chest, page 117):
Color: Royal Plum

Needles
1 US #8 [5.0 mm] 32-inch circular needle
1 US #8 [5.0 mm] 24-inch circular needle
1 set US #8 [5.0 mm] double pointed needles (optional)

Notions
Large stitch holder
Yarn needle
Stitch markers (including locking marker)
Waste yarn

Gauge
16 st /20 rows = 4 inches in St st
18 st/20 rows = 4 inches in pattern st
Change needles if necessary to achieve gauge

Substitutions
Madeline Tosh Vintage, Berroco Ultra Alpaca, Cascade Venezia

Pattern Notes

This shrug is worked side-to-side; the cast-on is at the center of the back. After the left back neck is worked, stitches are cast on for the left front. After the front ribbed border is worked, the front edge is shaped with short rows. The left front and back are then worked out to the side edge. The right back and front are worked in the same manner as the left but in the opposite direction, starting from the original cast-on. Before the sleeve is worked, the "side-seam sts" are grafted, leaving only the sleeve stitches on the needle. The sleeve is worked in the round to the cuff.

CR2 (coiled rib st): K the next st and leave it on the LH needle. Bring yarn to front and p the same st and the next st tog and drop both from LH needle. Bring yarn to back.

Coiled Rib Stitch Pattern
Row 1 (RS): K1, *CR2, k1; rep from * as specified in patt.
Row 2 (WS): Purl.
Rep [Row 1 and Row 2] for patt.

Note: When working Coiled Rib in the round, knit every other rnd.

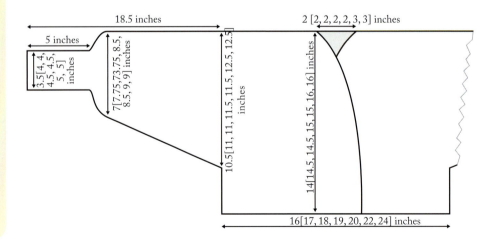

Pasarela

Instructions

With Judy's Magic Cast-On and longer circular needle, CO 71 (74, 74, 77, 77, 80, 80) stitches to each needle—142 (148, 148, 154, 154, 160, 160) total stitches.

Left Back

Note: Left Back is worked flat across one needle only. After you have worked the first several rows, you can move the sts from the resting needle to a holder or waste yarn.

Row 1 (WS): [P1, k1] 4 times, pm for lower border, p to last 8 sts, pm for shoulder, [k1, p1] 4 times.
Row 2 (RS): [K1, p1] 4 times, sm, k1, work Coiled Rib to marker, [p1, k1] 4 times.
Row 3: [P1, k1] 4 times, sm, p to next marker, sm, [k1, p1] 4 times.

Rep [Rows 2–3] until piece measures 1 (1, 1, 1, 1, 1.5, 1.5) inch(es) from CO, ending with a WS row.

Left Front and Back

With RS facing and using a knitted cast-on, CO an additional 62 (66, 66, 70, 70, 72, 72) sts—133 (140, 140, 147, 147, 152, 152) sts.

Row 1 (RS): * K1, p1; rep from * to first marker, sm, work Coiled Rib to next marker, sm, [p1, k1] 4 times.
Row 2: [P1, k1] 4 times, sm, p across to next marker, sm, [k1, p1] rep to end of row.

Rep [Rows 1–2] 4 (4, 4, 5, 5, 6, 6) times—8 (8, 8, 10, 10, 12, 12) rows total—on final repeat working Row 2 as follows for the indicated sizes:

Size 32: [P1, k1] 4 times, sm, M1P, p across to marker, sm, [k1, p1] 4 times.
Sizes 34, 36, 44, 48: Work Row 2 as written.
Sizes 38, 40: [P1, k1] 4 times, sm, p2tog, p across to marker, sm, [k1, p1] 4 times.

Left Front Short Row Shaping

Set-Up Row (RS): [K1, p1] 4 times, pm, work Coiled Rib to 12 sts before next marker (at shoulder), w&t.
Next Row and all WS rows: P to next marker, [k1, p1] 4 times.
Short Row (RS): [K1, p1] 4 times, sm, work in Coiled Rib to 3 sts before last wrapped st, w&t.

Rep Short-Row [every RS row] 11 more times, ending with a WS row.
Note: It is helpful to place a movable marker below the wrapped st that can be shifted to the wrapped st on the next RS row.

Next Row (RS): [K1, p1] 4 times, sm, working wrapped sts together with their wraps to conceal them, work Coiled Rib to next marker, rm, work Coiled Rib to next marker, sm, [p1, k1] 4 times.

Left Body

Row 1 (RS): [K1, p1] 4 times, sm, work Coiled Rib to next marker, sm, [p1, k1] 4 times.

Pasarela, Version 2
Shawl Pin: Plover Designs

Row 2 (WS): [P1, k1] 4 times, sm, p to next marker, sm, [k1, p1] 4 times.
Rep Rows [1–2] until back measures 8 (8.5, 9, 9.5, 10, 11, 12) inches from CO.

Cut yarn, leaving an 18-inch tail. Transfer all sts to a holder.

Right Back

With RS facing, join a new ball of yarn to the bottom edge of original cast-on.

Row 1 (RS): [K1, p1] 4 times, pm for lower border, work Coiled Rib to last 8 sts, pm, [p1, k1] 4 times. (Place a marker on this row to indicate the cast-on/midpoint for later measurements.)

Pasarela

Row 2 (WS): [P1, k1] 4 times, sm, purl to next marker, sm, [k1, p1] 4 times.

Rep [Rows 1–2] until piece measures 1 (1, 1, 1, 1, 1.5, 1.5) inch(es) ending with a RS row.

Right Front and back

With WS facing, cast on an additional 62 (66, 66, 70, 70, 72, 72) sts for Right Front using a knitted cast-on that is purled—133 (140, 140, 147, 147, 152, 152 sts.

Row 1(WS): *P1, k1; rep from* to first marker (at shoulder), sm, p to next marker, sm, [k1, p1] 4 times.
Row 2(RS): [K1, p1] 4 times, sm, work Coiled Rib to next marker, sm, *p1, k1; rep from * to end of row.

Rep [Rows 1–2] 4 (4, 4, 5, 5, 6, 6) times—8 (8, 8, 10, 10, 12, 12) rows total—on final repeat working Row 1 as follow for the indicated sizes:
Size 32: *p1, k1; rep from * to first marker (at shoulder), sm, p to next marker, M1P, sm, [k1, p1] 4 times.
Sizes 34, 36, 44, 48: Work Row 1 as written.
Sizes 38. 40: *P1, k1; rep from * to first marker (at shoulder), sm, p across to marker, p2tog, sm, [k1, p1] 4 times.

Right Front Short Row Shaping

Set-Up Row (WS): [P1, k1] 4 times, pm, p to 12 sts before next marker, w&t.

Return Row and all RS rows: Work Coiled Rib as est to next marker, sm, [p1, k1] 4 times.
Short Row (WS): [P1, k1] 4 times, sm, p to 3 sts before last wrapped stitch, w&t.

Rep Short Row [every WS row] 11 more times, ending with a RS row.

Next Row (WS): [P1, k1] 4 times, sm, working wrapped sts together with their wraps to conceal them p to shoulder marker, rm, p to next marker, sm, [k1, p1] 4 times.

Right Body

Row 1 (RS): [K1, p1] 4 times, sm, work Coiled Rib to next marker, sm, [p1, k1] 4 times.
Row 2 (WS): [P1, k1] 4 times, sm, p to next marker, sm, [k1, p1] 4 times.

Rep [Rows 1–2] until Right Back measures 8 (8.5, 9, 9.5, 10, 11, 12) inches from cast-on.
Cut yarn, leaving an 18" tail.

Right Sleeve

With RS facing fold entire piece at shoulder, bringing both needle ends together. Using Kitchener stitch and the tail, and beginning at the bottom edge, graft 17 sts from each needle. When finished there will be a k1 beginning on each side—100 (106, 106, 112, 112, 118, 118) sts on needle.

Transfer sts to a 24-in needle and join yarn at underarm; pm for BOR. Begin working in the round.
Rnd 1: Work Coiled Rib as est around.
Rnd 2: Knit around.
Rnd 3: Rep [Rnd 1].

Rnd 4 (dec): Sl 1, ssk, psso, k to last 3 sts, k2tog, sl next st over—96 (102, 102, 108, 108, 114, 114) sts.
Rnds 5 and 7: K1, work in est patt to last st, k1.
Rnd 6: Knit around.
Rnd 8 (dec): K1, ssk, k to last 3 sts, k2tog, k1—94 (100, 100, 106, 106, 112, 122) sts.

Repeat [Rnds 5–8] 15 more times—64 (70, 70, 76, 76, 82, 82) sts.

Sleeve Ribbing

Dec Rnd: *K1, k2tog; around—41 (47, 47, 53, 53, 59, 59) sts.
Rib Rnd: K1, * p1, k1; rep from * around.

Rep [Rib Rnd] for 5 inches (or to desired length).

BO loosely in pattern.

Left Sleeve

Work as for Right Sleeve.

Finishing

Fasten off and weave in all ends.

Pasarela

Above: Pasarela, Version 2

Left: Pasarela, Version 1
Shawl Pin: Tiggywinkle & Toolman

Garments & Wraps ⚓ Beyond Toes

November Street

Inspired by the arbor of old trees that line some of Portland's inner neighborhood streets, November Street is a wrap designed for using a heavier yarn than most shawls. Cascades of leaves invoking those blown in the autumn wind stream from the center. The stitch pattern is from Mitten, Pattern #11, found in "Home Work, a Choice Collection of Useful Designs for Crochet and Knitting Needle" [3], an 1891 publication. The wrap can be made in either small or large versions for any sized adult.

Duffy Stephens

November Street

Sizes
Small (Large)

Finished measurements
Length: 28 (40) inches
Width: 70 (120) inches

Yarn
Blue Moon Fiber Arts WooBu [60% merino wool, 40% Bambu; 620 yd/566 m per 8 oz/226 g skein]; 2 skeins
Version 1 (page 120):
Color: Pond Scum
Version 2 (page 123):
Color: KO - Going For Gold

Needles
2 US #8 [5 mm] 32-inch circular needles

Notions
Stitch markers
Yarn needle
Point protectors

Gauge
16 sts/20 rows = 4 inches in St st

Substitutions
Any light worsted-weight, solid or lightly marled yarn that is a blend of wool with silk, tencel, or bamboo.

Pattern Notes
This pattern is knitted from the center outward to the ends with decreases along one edge. Charts A and C show the repeat and surrounding stitches for each section.

On charts A and C, odd rows are wrong-side rows; even rows are right-side rows. On charts B and D, odd rows are right-side rows; even rows are wrong-side rows. The pattern is worked on both right and wrong sides.

Instructions
Using JMCO on two circular needles, CO 114 (147) sts to each needle—228 (294) total sts. Half of the sts will be held on one circular needle while you are working with the other for the first side of the wrap. Both sides are worked flat.

If desired, you may move the sts on the resting needle to a holder or to waste yarn while you work the first side.

Foundation Rows - First Side
Row 1F: Sl 1, k to end.
Row 2F: Sl 1, p to end.
Row 3F: P2, pm, [p2, yo, k1, yo, p2, k6, pm], rep to last 2 sts, p2.

First Side Pattern (Chart A)
Row 1 (WS): Sl 1, k1, [p4, p2tog tbl, k2, p3, k2] rep to last 2 sts, k2.
Row 2 (RS): Sl 1, p1, [p2, k1, yo, k1, yo, k1, p2, ssk, k3] rep to last 2 sts, p2.
Row 3: Sl 1, k1, [p2, p2tog tbl, k2, p5, k2] rep to last 2 sts, k2.
Row 4: Sl 1, p1, [p2, k2, yo, k1, yo, k2, p2, ssk, k1] rep to last 2 sts, p2.
Row 5: Sl 1, k1, [yo, p2tog tbl, yo, k2, p5, p2tog tbl, k2] rep to last 2 sts, k2.
Row 6: Sl 1, p1, [p2, ssk, k4, p2, k3] rep to last 2 sts, p2.
Row 7: Sl 1, k1, [p1, yo, p1, yo, p1, k2, p3, p2tog tbl, k2] rep to last 2 sts, k2.
Row 8: Sl 1, p1, [p2, ssk, k2, p2, k5] rep to last 2 sts, p2.
Row 9: Sl 1, k1, [p2, yo, p1, yo, p2, k2, p1, P2tog tbl, k2] rep to last 2 sts, RM, k2.
Row 10: Sl 1, p3, ssk, p2, ssk, k5, [p2, yo, ssk, yo, p2, ssk, k5] rep to last 2 sts, p2.
Row 11: Sl 1, k1, [p4, p2tog tbl, k2, p3, k2] rep to last 13 sts, p4, p2tog tbl, k2tog, k5.
Row 12: Sl 1, p1, p2tog, p2, ssk, k3, [p2, k1, yo, k1, yo, k1, p2, ssk, k3] rep to last 2 sts, p2.
Row 13: Sl 1, k1, [p2, p2tog tbl, k2, p5, k2] rep to last 9 sts, p2, p2tog tbl, k2tog, k3.
Row 14: Sl 1, p1, p2tog, ssk, k1, [p2, k2, yo, k1, yo, k2, p2, ssk, k1] rep to last 2 sts, p2.
Row 15: Sl 1, k1, [yo, p2tog tbl, yo, k2, p5, p2tog tbl, k2] rep to last 5 sts, p2tog tbl, k2tog, k1.
Row 16: Sl 1, p2tog, [p2, ssk, k4, p2, k3] rep to last 2 sts, p2.
Row 17: Sl 1, k1, [p1, yo, p1, yo, p1, k2, p3, p2tog tbl, k2] rep to last 2 sts, k2.

November Street

November Street, Version 2

Row 18: Sl 1, p1, [p2, ssk, k2, p2, k5] rep to last 2 sts, p2
Row 19: Sl 1, k1, [p2, yo, p1, yo, p2, k2, p1, p2tog tbl, k2] rep to last 2 sts, k2.
Row 20: Sl 1, p1, [p2, yo, ssk, yo, p2, ssk, k5] rep to last 2 sts, p2.

Rep Rows 1 - 20 until there are 30 sts left on your needle.

Work Rows 1 - 19 one more time, removing markers on row 19—17 sts.

Final Decrease rows (Chart B)
Row 1 (RS): Sl 1, p3, ssk, p2, ssk, k5, p2.
Row 2 (WS): Sl 1, k1, p4, p2tog tbl, k2tog, k5.
Row 3: Sl 1, p1, p2tog, p2, ssk, k3, p2.
Row 4: Sl 1, k1, p2, p2tog tbl, k2tog, k3.
Row 5: Sl 1, p1, p2tog, ssk, k1, p2.
Row 6: Sl 1, k1, p2tog tbl, k2tog, k1.
Row 7: Sl 1, p2tog. p2.
Row 8: Sl 1, k2tog, k1.
Row 9: Sl 1, p2tog.
Row 10: K2tog.

Break yarn. Thread end through loop and tighten.

If you moved the resting sts to a holder or waste yarn, return them to a circular needle. With WS facing, attach yarn.

Foundation Rows - Second Side
Row 1F (WS): Sl 1, purl to end.
Row 2F (RS): Sl 1, p1, PM [k6, p2, yo, k1, yo, p2, PM], rep to last 2 sts, p2.

Garments & Wraps ~ Beyond Toes

November Street

Left: November Street, Version 1; Right: November Street, Version 2

Second Side Pattern (Chart C)

Row 1 (WS): Sl 1, k1 [k2, p3, k2, p2tog, p4] rep to last 2 sts, k2.
Row 2 (RS): Sl 1, p1 [k3, k2tog, p2, k1, yo, k1, yo, k1, p2] rep to last 2 sts, p2.
Row 3: Sl 1, k1 [k2, p5, k2, p2tog, p2] rep to last 2 sts, k2.
Row 4: Sl 1, p1 [k1, k2tog, p2, k2, yo, k1, yo, k2, p2] rep to last 2 sts, p2.
Row 5: Sl 1, k1 [k2, p2tog, p5, k2, yo, p2tog, yo] rep to last 2 sts, k2.
Row 6: Sl 1, p1 [k3, p2, k4, k2tog, p2] rep to last 2 sts, p2.
Row 7: Sl 1, k1 [k2, p2tog, p3, k2, p1, yo, p1, yo, p1] rep to last 2 sts, k2.
Row 8: Sl 1, p1 [k5, p2, k2, k2tog, p2] rep to last 2 sts, p2.
Row 9: Sl 1, k1 [k2, p2tog, p1, k2, p2, yo, p1, yo, p2] rep to last 2 sts, K2.
Row 10: Sl 1, p1 [k5, k2tog, p2, yo, k2tog, yo, p2] rep to last 15 sts, k5, k2tog, p2, k2tog, p2, RM, p2.
Row 11: Sl 1, k4, ssk, p2tog, p4 [k2, p3, k2, p2tog, p4] rep to last 2 sts, k2.
Row 12: Sl 1, p1 [k3, k2tog, p2, k1, yo, k1, yo, k1, p2] rep to last 11 sts, k3, k2tog, p2, p2tog tbl, p2.
Row 13: Sl 1, k2, ssk, p2tog, p2 [k2, p5, k2, p2tog, p2] rep to last 2 sts, k2.
Row 14: Sl 1, p1, [k1, k2tog, p2, k2, yo, k1, yo, k2, p2] rep to last 7 sts, k1, k2tog, p2tog tbl, p2.
Row 15: Sl 1, ssk, p2tog, [k2, p2tog, p5, k2, yo, p2tog, yo] rep to last 2 sts, k2.
Row 16: Sl 1, p1, [k3, p2, k4, k2tog, p2] rep to last 3 sts, p2tog tbl, p1.
Row 17: Sl 1, k1 [k2, p2tog, p3, k2, p1, yo, p1, yo, p1] rep to last 2 sts, k2.
Row 18: Sl 1, p1, [k5, p2, k2, k2tog, p2] rep to last 2 sts, p2.
Row 19: Sl 1, k1, [k2, p2tog, p1, k2, p2, yo, p1, yo, p2] rep to last 2 sts, k2.
Row 20: Sl 1, p1, [k5, k2tog, p2, yo, k2tog, yo, p2] rep to last 2 sts, p2.

Rep Rows 1 - 20 until there are 30 sts left on your needle.
Work Rows 1 - 19 one more time, removing markers on row 19—17 sts.

Final Decrease Rows (Chart D)

Row 1: Sl 1, p1, k5, k2tog, p2, k2tog, p4.
Row 2: Sl 1, k4, ssk, p2tog, p4, k2 .
Row 3: Sl 1, p1, k3, k2tog, p2, p2tog tbl, p2.
Row 4: Sl 1, k2, ssk, p2tog, p2, k2.
Row 5: Sl 1, p1, k1, k2tog, p2tog tbl, p2.
Row 6: Sl 1, ssk, p2tog, k2.
Row 7: Sl 1, p1, p2tog, p1.
Row 8: Sl 1, ssk, k1.
Row 9: P2tog, p1.
Row 10: SSK.

Break yarn. Thread end through loop and tighten.

Finishing

Weave in ends. Block moderately to preserve the texture of the leaves against the purl background.

November Street

Chart A

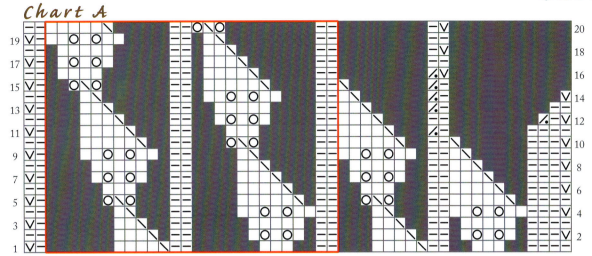

Chart C

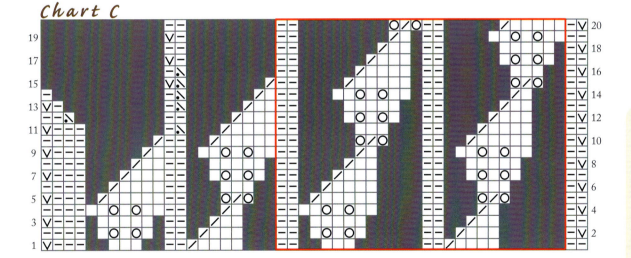

Chart D

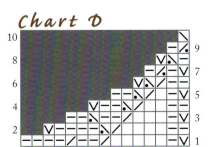

Chart B

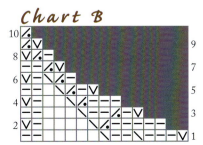

□	(RS) Knit, (WS) purl
—	(RS) Purl, (WS) knit
╱	(RS) K2tog, (WS) p2tog
╱.	(RS) P2tog, (WS) K2tog
╲	(RS) Ssk, (WS) p2tog tbl
╲.	(RS) P2tog tbl, (WS) ssk
O	Yo
V	Sl 1 with yarn held to WS
▢ (red)	Pattern repeat
■	No stitch

Garments & Wraps — Beyond Toes

125

Mokosh

Mokosh is the name of an ancient Slavic goddess associated with dispensing the water of life, shearing sheep, and spinning flax and wool. The pattern in this shawl reminds me of gentle ripples of water gliding towards shore and lapping eagerly against the sand. Worked from the center spine outwards to the tips, with the edging completed simultaneously with the body, this project flows quickly towards completion. A wonderful blending of wool and water that I think might suit Mokosh's sensibilities.

Cindy Abernethy

Mokosh

Finished Measurements
62 inches x 22 inches, blocked

Materials
Version 1 (page 126):
Blue Moon Fiber Arts Socks That Rock Lightweight [100% superwash merino wool; 360 yds/329 m per 4.5 oz/127 g skein]; color: Spinel; 2 skeins

Version 2 (page 129):
Blue Moon Fiber Arts Socks That Rock Lightweight [100% superwash merino wool; 360 yd/329 m per 4.5 oz/127 g skein]; color: Tanzanite; 2 skeins

Needles
2 US #5 [3.75 mm] 24-inch circular needles

Notions
2 stitch markers
Waste yarn (optional)
Darning needle to weave in ends

Gauge
20 sts/32 rows = 4 inches in St st after blocking

Substitutions
Fingering or sock-weight yarn in solid or semi-solid color

Pattern Notes

Use markers to indicate transitions between charts. In the written instructions, markers indicate transitions from stitches shown on one chart to the next. For example, in Row 1 of the first side, stitches from the beginning of the row to the first marker are shown on Chart A; stitches between the first and second marker are shown on Chart B; and stitches from the second marker to the end of the row are shown on Chart C. As you work, the shawl will decrease in width. Stitches for the final decrease section are shown on Chart D. For the second side, the markers indicate transitions from Charts E, F, and G, respectively, and stitches for the final decrease section are shown on Chart H.

On the first side, when binding off the stitches at the beginning of Chart A Row 17 and Chart D Rows 47, 49, and 51, place the last stitch back on the left hand needle before continuing.

On the first side, Row 1 starts at the bottom edge of the piece (the scalloped edging) and ends at the top edge with the garter lace border. On the second side, Row 1 begins at the garter lace border and ends at the bottom scalloped edging. Be careful to attach the yarn for the second side at the correct position.

On Chart H, a backward-loop cast on may be substituted when a row ends in a yo.

Instructions

Using two US #5 circular needles and JMCO, cast on 101 sts to each needle—202 stitches total.

The sts on the second needle may be left in place or moved to waste yarn. These sts will be worked for the second side of the shawl. Secure the ends of the needle or holder so no sts fall off while you work the first side of the shawl.

Continue by following either the written instructions on this page, or the charted instructions on page 132.

Written instructions

Row 1 (RS): [Yo, k2tog] twice, yo, ssk, k1, pm, p2tog tbl, p3, k2tog, yo, k1, [p5, k2tog, yo, k1] to last 6 sts, pm, k1, [yo, K2tog] twice, k1.

Row 2 (WS): K6, sm, [p3, k5] to last 7 sts before marker, p3, k4, sm, k6, kfb.

Row 3: [Yo, k2tog] twice, yo, ssk, k2, sm, p2tog tbl, p1, k2tog, yo, k2, [p4, k2tog, yo, k2] to next marker, sm, k1, [K2tog, yo] twice, k1.

Row 4: K6, sm, [p4, k4] to last 6 stitches before marker, p4, k2, sm, k7, kfb.

Row 5: [Yo, k2tog] 3 times, yo, ssk, k1, sm, k3tog tbl, yo, k3, [p3, k2tog, yo,

Mokosh

k3] to next marker, sm, k1, [yo, K2tog] twice, k1.

Row 6: K6, sm, [p5, k3] to 5 sts before marker, p5, sm, k8, kfb.

Row 7: [Yo, k2tog] 3 times, yo, ssk, k2, sm, ssk, k3, [p2, k2tog, yo, k4] to next marker, sm, k1, [k2tog, yo] twice, k1.

Row 8: K6, sm, [p6, k2] to last 4 sts before marker, p4, sm, k9, kfb.

Row 9: [Yo, k2tog] 4 times, yo, ssk, k1, sm, ssk, k2, [p1, k2tog, yo, k5] to next marker, sm, k1, [yo, k2tog] twice, k1.

Row 10: K6, sm, [p7, k1] to 3 sts before marker, p3, sm, k10, kfb.

Row 11: [Yo, k2tog] 4 times, yo, ssk, k2, sm, ssk, k1, [k2tog, yo, k6] to next marker, sm, k1, [k2tog, yo] twice, k1.

Row 12: K6, sm, p to next marker, sm, k11, kfb.

Row 13: [Yo, k2tog] five times, yo, ssk, k1, sm, ssk, [yo, k6, k2tog] to 8 sts before next marker, yo, k7, sm, k1, [yo, k2tog] twice, k1.

Row 14: K6, sm, p to next marker, sm, k12, kfb.

Row 15: [Yo, k2tog] 5 times, yo, ssk, k2, sm, k3tog tbl, k5, k2tog, yo, [k6, k2tog, yo] to 8 sts before next marker, k8, sm, k1, [k2tog, yo] twice, k1.

Row 16: K6, sm, p to next marker, sm, k13, kfb.

Row 17: BO 8, place last st back on LH needle, [yo, k2tog] twice, yo, ssk, k1, sm, yo, k3tog tbl, p5, [k1, yo, ssk, p5] to next marker, sm, k1, [yo, K2tog] twice, k1.

Row 18: K6, sm, [k5, p3] to 7 sts before marker, k5, p2, sm, k6, kfb.

Row 19: [Yo, k2tog] twice, yo, ssk, k2, sm, yo, k3tog tbl, p4, [k2, yo, ssk, p4] to next marker, sm, k1, [k2tog, yo] twice, k1.

Row 20: K6, sm, [k4, p4] to 6 sts before next marker, k4, p2, sm, k7, kfb.

Row 21: [Yo, k2tog] 3 times, yo, ssk, k1, sm, yo, k3tog tbl, p3, [k3, yo, ssk, p3] to next marker, sm, k1, [yo, k2tog] twice, k1.

Row 22: K6, sm, [k3, p5] to 5 sts before next marker, k3, p2, sm, k8, kfb.

Row 23: [Yo, k2tog] 3 times, yo, ssk, k2, sm, yo, k3tog tbl, p2, [k4, yo, ssk, p2] to next marker, sm, k1, [k2tog, yo] twice, k1.

Row 24: K6, sm, [k2, p6] to 4 sts before next marker, k2, p2, sm, k9, kfb.

Row 25: [Yo, k2tog] 4 times, yo, ssk, k1, sm, yo, k3tog tbl, p1, [k5, yo, ssk, p1] to next marker, sm, k1, [yo, k2tog] twice, k1.

Row 26: K6, sm, [k1, p7] to 3 sts before next marker, k1, p2, sm, k10, kfb.

Row 27: [Yo, k2tog] 4 times, yo, ssk, k2, sm, yo, k3tog tbl, [k6, yo, ssk] to 8 sts before next marker, k8, sm, k1, [k2tog, yo] twice, k1.

Row 28: K6, sm, p to next marker, sm, k11, kfb.

Row 29: [Yo, k2tog] 5 times, yo, ssk, k1, sm, yo, k3tog tbl, yo, [ssk, k6, yo] to 8 sts before next marker, ssk, k7, sm, k1, [yo, k2tog] twice, k1.

Row 30: K6, sm, p to next marker, sm, k12, kfb.

Row 31: [Yo, k2tog] 5 times, yo, ssk, k2, sm, yo, k3tog tbl, k6, [yo, ssk, k6] to next marker, sm, k1, [k2tog, yo] twice, k1.

Row 32: K6, sm, p to next marker, sm, k13, kfb.

Row 33: BO 8 st, place last st back on LH needle, [yo, k2tog] twice, yo, ssk, k1, sm, p2tog tbl, p3, k2tog, yo, k1, [p5, k2tog, yo, k1] to last 6 sts, sm, k1, [yo, K2tog] twice, k1.

Rep [Rows 2–33].

Mokosh, Version 2
Shawl Pin: Plover Designs

Garments & Wraps — Beyond Toes

Mokosh

Each time you complete one rep, you'll decrease 1 8-st section of the main body pattern (the span of stitches between the markers).

On the last rep of these 32 rows, the middle section sts in brackets will not be used, and at the end of Row 33, you should have 20 sts on your needle and be ready to work a WS row.

Mokosh, Version 2
shawl Pin: Plover Designs

Finish the first side by working Rows 34–52, removing markers as you come to them.

Row 34: K6, p3, k10, kfb.
Row 35: [Yo, k2tog] twice, yo, ssk, k2, p2tog tbl, p1, k2tog, yo, k3, [yo, k2tog] twice, k1.
Row 36: K6, p4, k9, kfb.
Row 37: [Yo, k2tog] 3 times, yo, ssk, k1, k3tog tbl, yo, k4, [k2tog, yo] twice, k1.
Row 38: K6, p5, k8, kfb.
Row 39: [Yo, k2tog] 3 times, yo, ssk, k2, ssk, k4, [yo, k2tog] twice, k1.
Row 40: K6, p4, k9, kfb.
Row 41: [Yo, k2tog] 4 times, yo, ssk, k1, ssk, k3, [k2tog, yo] twice, k1.
Row 42: K6, p3, k10, kfb.
Row 43: [Yo, k2tog] 4 times, yo, ssk, k2, ssk, k2, [yo, k2tog] twice, k1.
Row 44: K6, p2, k11, kfb.
Row 45: [Yo, k2tog] 5 times, yo, ssk, [yo, k2tog] 4 times, yo, k1.
Row 46: K to last st, kfb.
Row 47: BO 8 sts, place last st back on LH needle, ssk, [yo, k2tog] 6 times, k1.
Row 48: Knit
Row 49: BO 5 st, place last st back on LH needle, ssk, k1, [ssk, yo] twice, yo, k1.
Row 50: K6, k2tog.
Row 51: BO 3 st, place last st back on LH needle, ssk, k2.
Row 52: K3tog, cut yarn and pull through loop of last st.

You are halfway there!

Second Side

Turn your work. If you left the stitches on waste yarn, return them to a needle. Begin with Row 1 of the instructions.

Row 1 (RS): P1, [p2tog tbl, yo] twice, p1, pm, [p1, yo, ssk, k5] to last 15 sts, p1, yo, ssk, k3, p2tog, pm, p1, p2tog, yo, [p2togtbl, yo] twice.
Row 2 (WS): Kfb, p6, sm, p6, k1, [p7, k1] to next marker, sm, p6.
Row 3: P1, [yo, p2tog tbl] twice, p1, sm, [p2, yo, ssk, k4] to 7 sts before next marker, p2, yo, ssk, k1, p2tog, sm, p2, p2tog, yo, [p2tog tbl, yo] twice.
Row 4: Kfb, p7, sm, p4, k2, [p6, k2] to next marker, sm, p6.
Row 5: P1, [p2tog tbl, yo] twice, p1, sm, [p3, yo, ssk, k3] to 6 s before next marker, p3, yo, p3tog, sm, p1, p2tog, yo, [p2tog tbl, yo] 3 times.
Row 6: Kfb, p8, sm, p2, k3, [p5, k3] to next marker, sm, p6.
Row 7: P1, [yo, p2tog tbl] twice, p1, sm, [p4, yo, ssk, k2] to 5 sts before next marker, p3, p2tog, sm, p2, p2tog, yo, [p2tog tbl, yo] 3 times.
Row 8: Kfb, p9, sm, p1, k3, [p4, k4] to next marker, sm, p6.
Row 9: P1, [p2tog tbl, yo] twice, p1, sm, [p5, yo, ssk, k1] to 4 sts before next marker, p2, p2tog, sm, p1, p2tog, yo, [p2tog tbl, yo] 4 times.
Row 10: Kfb, p10, sm, p1, k2, [p3, k5] to next marker, sm, p6.

Mokosh

Row 11: P1, [yo, p2tog tbl] twice, p1, sm, [p6, yo, ssk] to 3 sts before next marker, p1, p2tog, sm, p2, p2tog, yo, [p2tog tbl, yo] 4 times.

Row 12: Kfb, p11, sm, p1, k1, [p2, k6] to next marker, sm, p6.

Row 13: P1, [p2tog tbl, yo] twice, p1, sm, p7, yo, [ssk, p6, yo] to 3 sts before next marker, p3tog, sm, p1, p2tog, yo, [p2tog tbl, yo] 5 times.

Row 14: Kfb, p12, sm, p2, k7, [p1, k7] to next marker, sm, p6.

Row 15: P1, [yo, p2tog tbl] twice, p1, sm, p8, [yo, ssk, p6] to 9 sts before next marker, yo, ssk, p5, p2tog, sm, p2, p2tog, yo, [p2tog tbl, yo] 4 times, p2tog tbl.

Row 16: BO 6 sts, p6, sm, p1, k5, p2, [k6, p2] to 8 sts before next marker, k8, sm, p6.

Row 17: P1, [p2tog tbl, yo] twice, p1, sm, [k5, k2tog, yo, p1] to last 8 sts, k5, k3tog, yo, sm, p1, p2tog, yo, [p2togtbl, yo] twice.

Row 18: Kfb, p6, sm, p7,[k1, p7] to next marker, sm, p6.

Row 19: P1, [yo, p2tog tbl] twice, p1, sm, [k4, k2tog, yo, p2] to 7 sts before next marker, k4, k3tog, yo, sm, p2, p2tog, yo, [p2tog tbl, yo] twice.

Row 20: Kfb, p7, sm, p6, [k2, p6] to next marker, sm, p6.

Row 21: P1, [p2tog tbl, yo] twice, p1, sm, [k3, k2tog, yo, p3] to 6 sts before next marker, k3, k3tog, yo, sm, p1, p2tog, yo, [p2tog tbl, yo] 3 times.

Row 22: Kfb, p8, sm, p5,[k3, p5] to next marker, sm, p6.

Row 23: P1, [yo, p2tog tbl] twice, p1, sm, [k2, k2tog, yo, p4] to 5 sts before next marker, k2, k3tog, yo, sm, p2, p2tog, yo, [p2tog tbl, yo] 3 times.

Row 24: Kfb, p9, sm, p4, [k4, p4] to next marker, sm, p6.

Row 25: P1, [p2tog tbl, yo] twice, p1, sm, [k1, k2tog, yo, p5] to 4 sts before next marker, k1, k3tog, yo, sm, p1, p2tog, yo, [p2tog tbl, yo] 4 times.

Row 26: Kfb, p10, sm, p3, [k5, p3] to next marker, sm, p6.

Row 27: P1, [yo, p2tog tbl] twice, p1, sm, [k2tog, yo, p6] to 3 sts before next marker, k3tog, yo, sm, p2, p2tog, yo, [p2tog tbl, yo] 4 times.

Row 28: Kfb, p11, sm, p2, [k6, p2] to next marker, sm, p6.

Row 29: P1, [p2tog tbl, yo] twice, p1, sm, p7, k2tog, [yo, p6, k2tog] to 9 sts before next marker, yo, p6, k3tog, yo, sm, p1, p2tog, yo, [p2tog tbl, yo] 5 times.

Row 30: Kfb, p12, sm, [p2, k6] to 9 sts before next marker, p2, k7, sm, p6.

Row 31: P1, [yo, p2tog tbl] twice, p1, sm, [p6, k2tog, yo] to 9 sts before next marker, p6, k3tog, yo, sm, p2, p2tog, yo, [p2tog tbl, yo] 4 times, p2tog tbl.

Row 32: BO 6 sts, p6, sm, [p2, k6] to next marker, sm, p6.

Repeat [Rows 1–32].

`Each time you complete one repeat, you'll decrease 1 8-st section of the main body pattern.

On the last repeat of these 32 rows, the middle section sts in brackets will not be used, and at the end of row 32, you should have 21 sts on your needle and be ready to work a RS row.

Finish the second side by working Rows 33–52, removing markers as you come to them.

Row 33: P1, [p2tog tbl, yo] twice, p2, yo, ssk, k3, p2tog, p1, p2tog, yo, [p2tog tbl, yo] twice.

Row 34: Kfb, p12, k1, p6

Row 35: P1, [yo, p2tog tbl] twice, p3, yo, ssk, k1, p2tog, p2, p2tog, yo, [p2tog tbl, yo] twice.

Row 36: Kfb, p11, k2, p6.

Row 37: P1, [p2tog tbl, yo] twice, p4, yo, p3tog, p1, p2tog, yo, [p2tog tbl, yo] 3 times.

Row 38: Kfb, p10, k3, p6.

Row 39: P1, [yo, p2tog tbl] twice, p4, p2tog, p2, p2tog, yo, [p2tog tbl, yo] 3 times.

Row 40: Kfb, p10, k3, p6.

Row 41: P1, [p2tog tbl, yo] twice, p3, p2tog, p1, p2tog, yo [p2tog tbl, yo] 4 times.

Row 42: Kfb, p11, k2, p6

Row 43: P1, [yo, p2tog tbl] twice, p2, p2tog, p2, p2tog, yo, [p2tog tbl, yo] 4 times.

Row 44: Kfb, p12, k1, p6

Row 45: P1, [p2tog tbl, yo] twice, p1, [p2tog, yo] 3 times, [p2tog tbl, yo] 4 times, p1.

Row 46: BO 7 sts purlwise, p13.

Row 47: P1, [yo, p2tog tbl] twice, p1, [yo, p2tog tbl] 3 times, yo, p2tog.

Mokosh

Row 48: BO 5 in purlwise, p8.
Row 49: P1, [p2tog tbl, yo] twice, p2, p2tog.
Row 50: BO 3 in purlwise, p3.
Row 51: P2, p2tog.
Row 52: P3tog, cut yarn and pull through loop of last stitch.

Charted Instructions

First Side

Row 1: Work Row 1 of Chart A; pm; Row 1 of Chart B, repeating the 8-st section outlined in red to last 6 sts of row; pm; Row 1 of Chart C to end.
Row 2: Work Row 2 of Chart C; sm; Row 2 of Chart B, repeating the 8-st section outlined in red to next marker; sm; Row 2 of Chart A to end.

Continue following charts in this manner, slipping markers as you come to them.

1 rep of Chart B = 2 reps of Chart A = 8 repeats of Chart C.

Note: Row 1 of Chart A is a set-up row and is not included in the repeat.
Each time you complete 1 rep of Chart B, you'll decrease one 8-stitch section of the main body pattern (Chart B). When 20 sts remain on your needle and you're ready to work a WS row, finish the first side by following Chart D, removing markers as you come to them.

Second Side

Row 1 (RS): With RS facing, work Row 1 of Chart E; pm; Row 1 of Chart F, repeating the 8-st section outlined in red to last 14 stitches of row; pm; Row 1 of Chart G to end.
Row 2: Work Row 2 of Chart G; sm; Row 2 of Chart F, repeating the 8-st section outlined in red to next marker; sm; Row 2 of Chart E to end.

Continue following charts in this manner, slipping markers as you come to them.
1 rep of Chart F = 8 reps of Chart E = 2 reps of Chart G.

Each time you complete one rep of Chart F, you'll decrease one 8-st section of the main body pattern (Chart F). When 21 sts remain on your needle and you're ready to work a RS row, finish the second side by following Chart H, removing markers as you come to them.

Finishing

Weave in the ends, block, and enjoy.

☐	Knit (RS), purl (WS)
⊟	Purl (RS), knit (WS)
O	Yo
╱	K2tog (RS), Ssp (WS)
╲	Ssk (RS) P2tog (WS)
⌒	Bind off
	Kfb (RS), pfb (WS)
	Pfb (RS), kfb (WS)
	Purl 3 sts together
	P2tog (RS), SSK (WS)
	Ssp (RS), K2tog (WS)
	Knit 3 sts together
	Knit 3 sts together tbl
■	No stitch
☐	Pattern repeat

Mokosh

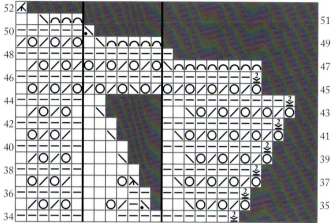

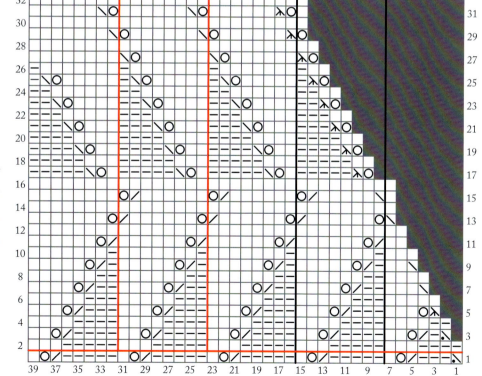

Garments & Wraps ⚓ Beyond Toes

Mokosh

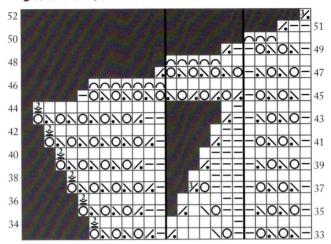

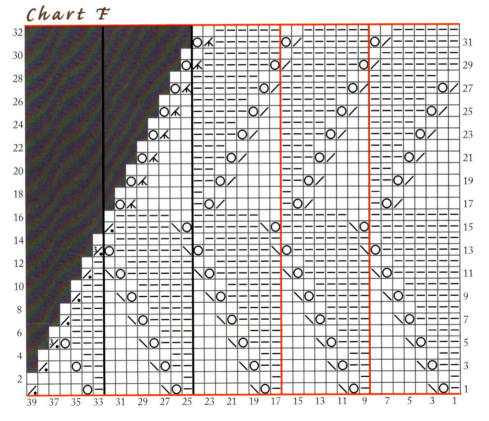
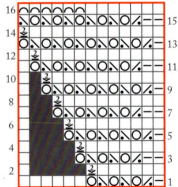

Beyond Toes ⚓ Garments & Wraps

Mokosh

Mokosh, Version 1
Shawl Pin: Plover Designs

Garments & Wraps ⟋ Beyond Toes

136

Poncho Puzzle

Where does it start? Where does it end? How does it get from here to there without any seams? I love to construct things that make other knitters go "Hmmmm......how did she do that?" but aren't really that complicated. You know, the things that make you say, "Now why didn't I think of that?" This is hopefully one of those.

Joan Schrouder

Poncho Puzzle

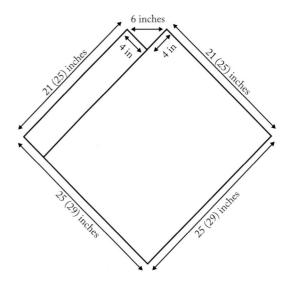

Sizes
Small (Large)

Finished Measurements:
Each rectangle measures approximately 21 (25) inches by 29 (33) inches before joining and adding trim

Yarn
Noro Kureyon [100% wool; 109 yd/100 m per 50 g skein]

Version 1 (small, page 136, left):
Color 233; 8 skeins

Version 2 (large, page 136, right):
Color 185; 10 skeins

Needles
Two US #10.5 [6.5 mm] 40-inch circular needles

Two US #10.5 [6.5 mm] 16-inch or shorter size circular needles for twined I-cord

Notions
Markers - 5 that open, e.g. safety pin-type

Blunt darning needle with large eye

2 or 4 pieces of waste yarn about 6 inches long each for provisional I-cord cast on. You can reuse the 2 pieces if you wish.

Gauge
10 sts/16 rows = 3 inches in St st after blocking

Gauge need not be exact as poncho fit isn't crucial.

Substitutions:
Any wool yarn with long color changes that has approximately 100 m per 50 g. If a non-wool yarn is used, it should be bulkier to maintain shape.

Pattern Notes

Before starting rewind each ball of the Noro. This allows you to see the progression of the colors. First, choose 2 balls to hold back for the I-cord trim. Picking balls that progress through different colors at the same points will provide more contrast when working the two I-cords.

Then examine the remaining balls and note the beginning and ending colors of each. If you want to start each new ball with the same or similar color as the previous one left off, divvy them up for use between the 2 rectangles in the sequence to be used. You also have the option of starting some balls from the center and others from the outside yarns. Or chose to eliminate some colors if they're not your favorites. Noro wool spit-splices easily so you can break and join back in without leaving a lot of tails to darn in later.

The smaller version uses 3 skeins for each rectangle plus 1 skein for trim. The larger version uses 4 skeins for each rectangle plus 2 skeins for trim. An extra skein is recommended to have more color options and allow for gauge differences in the trim.

The neck size will remain the same for both versions. The diagram above shows the size after joining, before the trim has been added.

You may change from 2 circular needles to Magic Loop at any point after the first round, and continue with Magic Loop until there are enough stitches to slide comfortably around the needle without any loops. This is approximately at the 120 stitches stage for a 40-inch needle.

Poncho Puzzle

Instructions

Using JMCO and both long circular needles, CO 32 sts to each needle—64 sts total.

Rnd 1: *M1R, k1, M1R, k31, rep from * once.
Rnd 2: K around.

As you knit each M1 from previous row, put a marker into the base of it. These will be your corner sts. Put another marker into the first marker to designate the beg of the rnd.

Rnd 3: *K1, M1R, k to next marked st, M1L, rep from * 3 more times—76 sts. 8 sts. inc, 1 on each side of marked/corner sts in pairs of M1s.
Rnd 4: K around.

Rep [Rnds 3 and 4] until rectangle is 18 (21) inches by 27 (30) inches. Approximately 3 (4) balls of yarn used up.

Do not cut the yarn.

Set aside the live sts still on the needle and make a second rectangle the same way on the second needle, using one of the shorter needles for the second circ needle during the cast on. Switch over to the long needle used as Magic Loop after the first rnd.

Note: Second rectangle must have the same number of stitches on each side as first rectangle. The poncho can be made larger or smaller by knitting more or fewer rounds on both rectangles provided the stitch count on each is the same.

Joining Rectangles

Lay out both rectangles with RS facing you, matching a short side of one to a long side of the other, both meeting at the edges on your right in an inverted L-shape (see diagram).

Break yarn still attached to the bottom rectangle leaving an approximately 45-inch long tail as shown. Thread the tail on a blunt darning needle and weave the live sts from the short side of the bottom rectangle to the corresponding live sts of the long side of the rectangle above it using Kitchener st, working right to left for right-handers. If you weave left-handed, after orienting the rectangles as above, turn both pieces together as a unit upside down and work from left to right at same point.

After one side is grafted and Kitchener sts adjusted to same size as other knitted rows, pull remaining short and long sides tog as before and repeat the grafting there. The live sts remaining ungrafted in the center will become the neckline.

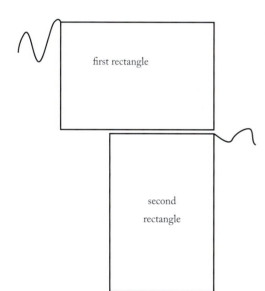

Poncho Puzzle; Left: Version 2; Right: Version 1

Poncho Puzzle

Twisted I-Cord Trim For Neck Edge

You will be knitting with the same side always facing, going from the 3rd st back to the first st while pulling yarn snugly behind the needle.

Using one short circular needle, CO 3 sts with a short piece of waste yarn. Do not turn the needle but switch it to your other hand. Slide sts back to other end.

Drop waste yarn and begin working with main yarn.

Work attached I-cord: *K2, SSK the 3rd st tog with a live st from the neck edge. Sl the 3 sts back purlwise to LH needle. Rep from * 2 more times—3 sts of neck edge have been bound off.

Work unattached I-cord on same sts: *K 3 sts, sl back to LH needle; rep from * 6 more times—7 unattached I-cord rows. Do not slip the 3 sts back to LH needle. Instead, push needle holding these 3 sts to back of work.

Start second I-cord the same way using the second short needle. Work attached I-cord as above, attaching to the next 3 live sts from the neckline.

Then work 7 rows of unattached I-cord as above. Push this second needle to the back, out of the way.

Bring the first I-cord back over the second cord and work attached I-cord for 3 rows, then work unattached I-cord for 7 rows, then put to the back out of the way.

Keep alternating the 2 I-cords, always bringing the new one over the old one when alternating to keep the twist going in the same direction.

On the last unattached segment with each color, work 6 rows, then break the yarn leaving a 6-inch tail.

Thread on the darning needle and graft the last 3 sts over the waste yarn of the beg of that I-cord, following the contrasting color of the waste yarn until the graft is complete. Pull out the waste yarn and the graft should appear seamless. Rep the same ending for the other I-cord. Adjust tension of grafting as needed.

Twisted I-cord Trim For Body Edge

Starting at one corner, beg the two I-cords as for neck. Work alternating attached and unattached I-cord as for neck until you come to the next corner. Then work 10 rows unattached for each color to give extra length for the corners. If you're working 1-2 fewer rows than 7 unattached, then likewise work 2-3 fewer rows for corners, too.

Graft ends of I-cord to beginnings and remove waste yarns.

It's also fine to always bring the new cord under the old one to twist in the opposite direction, but do pick one way and then stick to it. Attachments happen in 3-stitch increments and there are 2 colors. If you have a number of sts that isn't evenly divisible by 6, you may need to attach to only 2 sts once or 4 sts once with either or both colors. Do so as needed; it's not highly visible.

The I-cord may look pretty loose and stringy as worked, but will fluff up and fill out after washing. If your row gauge is longer than specified in the pattern, i.e., you have fewer rows than indicated in gauge info, then work a row or 2 fewer unattached rows so they don't end up too long.

Blocking

Soak in very warm, sudsy water with 1/2 cup of white vinegar in sink for 30 minutes. Don't agitate but push gently through water a few times at first to make sure it's totally submerged. Drain and squeeze out most of the water. Refill sink with same temperature water, now moderately warm, to which a couple of capfuls of hair conditioner have been added. Soak 30 minutes. Drain, squeeze out and rinse well. Put through spin cycle in washer.

Lay flat to dry on towels, smoothing to shape and size. Turn over on fresh towels after 4-8 hours and let dry on other side.

Blockalicious

I love bags. I was knitting purses with lovely cable designs and twisted stitch designs but the finished item always needed to be lined to be truly usable. Then I discovered felting. My first design was a shoulder "spare pocket", just big enough for keys and phone. Next I went big and knit a monster carryall. I then settled down to create project bags for all my unfinished objects. Many sizes and shapes later, I found my square. It is just right for a pair of socks or lace project and it sits so nicely right next to me while I am working. I always place a pocket (or two) in my projects, to keep things organized. Mosaic knitting and felting are a wonderful combination for creating a totally unique object.

Nadine Foster

Blockalicious

Finished Measurements
After felting, approximately 6.5 inches long x 6.5 inches wide x 6.5 inches tall

Yarn
Version 1 (page 142):
Patons Classic Wool [100% wool; 223 yd/205 m per 100 g skein]
[MC] Royal Purple; 1 skein
[CC#] Lemongrass; 1 skein

Version 2:
Cascade 220 [100% Peruvian highland wool; 220 yd/200 m per 100 g/3.5 oz skein]
[MC} #8555 (Black); 1 skein
[CC] #7816 (Bluebell); 1 skein

Needles
1 US #10.5 [6.5 mm] 29-inch circular needle
2 US #10.5 [6.5 mm] 16-inch circular needles
OR
1 set US #10.5 [6.5 mm] double-pointed needles

Notions
3 stitch markers for corners
1 distinct stitch marker for beginning of round
Tapestry needle

Gauge
16 sts/20 rows = 4 inches in St st
(Gauge is not so important in felted projects)

Substitutions
Any worsted-weight yarn that will felt well.

Pattern Notes
This project uses only the knit stitch.

The chart is mosaic knitting which uses only one color per row; the two-color pattern is formed by slipping stitches from the previous rounds, thereby bringing the unused color up to the current round. The color to be knit is shown on the chart column to the right of the row number. All stitches of the other color are slipped as if to purl with the yarn held in back of the work. Each color is worked for two rounds and the second round of the color is always exactly the same as the first round of that color.

Do not cut either MC or CC yarn until the entire chart has been worked. When switching colors, carry the yarn loosely up on the wrong side of the work.

Instructions
Using Judy's Magic Cast-On with Main Color and either longer circular needle or two shorter circular needles, cast on 28 sts to each needle—56 sts total.

Bottom
The bottom is worked flat in garter st. Turn needles so the purl bumps are facing you (see instructions for garter stitch in *Knitting From Both Directions—Provisional Bay*, page 16). You will work across the 28 sts on Needle 1 while the remaining 28 sts rest.

Row 1: Sl 1, k27, turn;
Rep Row 1 until there are 28 garter ridges and the top and reserved needles have the purl bumps next to the needle on the "right" side.

Sides
The sides are worked in the round. If you cast on using 2 shorter circular needles, you may find it easier to switch to the longer circular needle now.

Set-up Rnd: Continuing with MC, pm (beginning of round), k28, pm, pick up and knit 28 sts using the loops provided by the slipped sts, pm, k28, pm, pick up and knit 28 sts on the remaining edge again using the loops from the slipped sts—112 sts.

K 6 rnds of MC.

On the next rnd, begin working the chart. The chart will be repeated four times around, once for each side of the block. Complete all chart rnds.

K 2 rnds of MC.

Upon completion of the chart, the CC working thread may be cut. The end can be slipped in and out of the corner sts on the inside to reinforce the corners. (I

Blockalicious

occasionally place additional yarn lengths in the corners for support.)

You may choose either the Twisted I-Cord Trim (shown on Version 1), or the Wavy I-Cord Trim (shown on Version 2).

Twisted I-cord Trim Setup
I-cord segment: Using 16-inch circular needle or dpns and the MC, CO 3 sts, [slide sts to the other end of the needle, k3] 6 times; [sl sts to the circular needle holding the project, k2, k2tog (I-cord attached)] 4 times. Hold needle to back of work.

Rep I-cord segment using CC.

Wavy I-cord Trim Setup
I-cord segment: Using 16-inch circular needle or dpns and the MC, CO 3 sts, [slide sts to the other end of the needle, k3] 6 times; [sl sts to the circular needle holding the project, k2, k2tog (I-cord attached)] once. Hold needle to back of work.

Repeat I-cord segment using CC.

Both Trims
Place the 2nd needle to the back and bring the first needle forward (always bring the new one over the previous one); with MC work another I-cord segment as specified for trim type.

Continue rotating the 2 needles, alternating MC and CC I-cord segments, until

Blockalicious, Version 1

all the sts on the long circular needle have been worked. Using the tapestry needle, carefully making sure the twists are correct, locate the beginning and end of each matching I-cord, and graft the 2 ends together using Kitchener st.

Pocket (optional)
Turn work inside out. Slide circular needle into one of the rows at the base of any side, picking up 28 sts.

Knit in garter st until the pocket reaches the top of the mosaic pattern (about 6 inches).

BO in attached I-Cord: Using CC, CO 3 sts with the backwards loop CO. * K2, k2tog, sl all sts back to the left needle, rep from * until all pocket sts have been worked. [K2tog] twice and pull the working yarn through.

Sew the side edges of the pocket to the inside corners of the box. Then take a length of yarn equal to the 3 sides of the pocket and using the tapestry needle, weave it in and out right at the seam around the pocket. This makes a denser seam when felted.

Blockalicious

I-cord Handles
Using 16-inch circular needle or dpns, CO 3 sts. * Slide the sts to the opposite end of the needle, k3, rep from * until I-cord measures approximately 12 inches long. [K2tog] twice and pull the working yarn through.

Rep for second handle.

Attach each end of the handles to one of the corners by sewing them in. The felting will hide the sewing stitches.

Finishing
Soak the project in hot water in a sink for about 30 minutes with a drop of liquid dish-washing soap or shampoo. Carefully squeeze out the water and take the project to the washer.

Set the washer to hot wash/cold rinse. To the water in the washer add ¼ cup baking soda and ½ cup Boraxo. Throw in some old jeans or towels with the project. This encourages the felting process.

In my front loader, it usually takes one regular cycle and one short cycle to meet my desired level of felting. I prefer that my stitches do not show.

To block my projects while drying, I find items in the house that have the same dimensions I want. You can also make your own blocking form using cardboard.

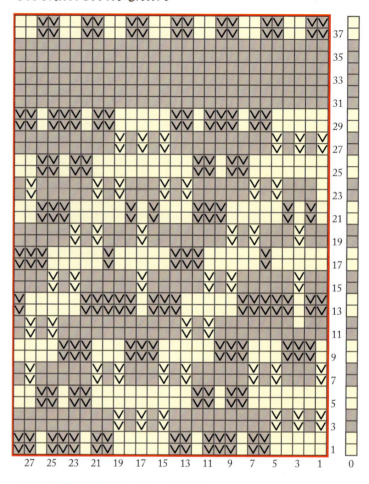

Blockalicious

Blockalicious, Version 2

Bags & Cozies ~ Beyond Toes

148

Cabled Netbook Cozy

This cozy cabled cover for your mini-laptop or "netbook" starts with Judy's Magic Cast-On to create a gusset and then is worked in the round on two circular needles. The simple cable pattern radiates from the center and is suitable for beginners, as well as being a great first chart-reading project. The top is finished with applied i-cord to make installing the zipper a breeze. The piece can also be adapted to fit larger notebook computers or made slightly thinner to accommodate an e-reader or iPad. Special thanks to my friend Ilene, whose pullover with radiating cables was the inspiration for this design.

Kendra Nitta

Cabled Netbook Cozy

Finished Measurements (flat)
Width: 8 inches
Length: 11 inches

Yarn
Blue Sky Alpacas Organic Cotton [100% organic cotton; 150 yd/137 m per 100 g skein]; 1 skein

Version 1 (modified to fit smaller netbook—page 148):
Color: 81–Sand

Version 2 (unmodified—page 151):
Color: 82–Nut

The project uses almost one skein of yarn. If the dimensions of your netbook are slightly larger, or if you would prefer not to unravel your swatch, purchase a second skein of yarn.

Needles
2 US #7 [4.5 mm] 24-inch circular needles

Notions
St markers (optional, use if working on one needle instead of two)
1 locking st marker
Tapestry needle
Nylon invisible zipper, 16-inches
Sewing thread to match yarn
Sewing needle
2 pieces of cardboard cut to the size of the netbook and covered with foil (for blocking)

Gauge
18 sts/28 rows = 4 inches in St st
21 sts/28 rows = 4 inches in pattern st (unblocked)

Substitutions
Malabrigo Organic Cotton
Any superwash worsted-weight wool

Pattern Notes

This pattern is written to fit a netbook computer that is approximately 10 inches long, 6.5 inches wide, and about 1 inch thick. If your netbook has different dimensions, basic instructions for adapting the pattern are included. The finished piece includes a gusset a little less than 1 inch wide to accommodate the thickness of the netbook. To adapt the pattern for an e-reader or thinner netbook, omit one stitch on each side of the gusset.

You will notice that the piece biases considerably before blocking. In addition, the center section of the gusset may bulge out a bit. This is normal and will be corrected in blocking. Before blocking, cut two pieces of cardboard the same dimensions as your netbook. Place enough newspaper or bubble wrap between the cardboard to match the thickness of your netbook. Tape together, and then cover with tin foil. Use this blocking form to block piece to the right dimensions.

Special stitch instructions:

C3b (cable 3 back): Sl 2 sts to cn and hold in back, k1, k2 sts from cn.
C3f (cable 3 front): Sl 1 to cn and hold in front, k2, k st from cn.
C5b (cable 5 back): Sl 3 to cn and hold in back, k2, sl st from cn back to LH needle and purl, k2 from cn.
C5f (cable 5 front): Sl 3 to cn and hold in front, k2, sl st from cable needle back to LH needle and purl, k2 from cable needle.

Instructions

Body
Using two 24-inch circular needles and Judy's Magic Cast-On, CO 6 sts to each needle—12 st total.

Working sts on Needle 1 only:
Rows 1 and 3 (RS): P1, k4, p1.
Rows 2 and 4: K1, p4, k1.

Setup for working in the rnd:
With Needle 1 and RS facing, p1, k4, p1; pick up and knit 1 st in (not under) the purl bump in the center of selvage; rep for sts on Needle 2—14 sts.

Redistribute the first 3 sts from Needle 1 to Needle 2, and the last 3 sts from Needle 2 to Needle 1, so that the picked-up st is in the center of each needle, and the original 6 sts are equally divided between the two needles. Transfer the 3 unworked sts on Needle 2 from the RH side to the LH side of Needle 2; p1, k2.

Place a locking st marker on the sts on Needle 1 to identify Needle 1.

Rnd 1: [K2, p1, k1, p1, k2] twice.
Rnd 2: [K2, M1T, p1, CDI, p1, M1A, k2] twice—22 sts.

Cabled Netbook Cozy

Increase rnds
Follow either the written instructions below or the charts on pages 154 and 155. If working from the charts, work line 1 of Chart A, then line 1 of Chart B on Needle 1; rep for Needle 2.

Note: The st count is the total number of sts on both needles.

Written Instructions
Rnd 1: * K2, [M1T, k1, p1, k1, M1A, k1] twice, k1, rep from * on Needle 2—30 sts.

Rnd 2: * K4, p1, k5, p1, k4, rep from * on Needle 2.

Rnd 3: * K2, [M1T, k2, p1, k2, M1A, k1] twice, k1, rep from * on Needle 2—38 sts.

Rnd 4: * [K2, p1] three times, k1, [p1, k2] three times, rep from * on Needle 2.

Rnd 5: * K2, [M1T, p1, k2, p1, k2, p1, M1A, k1] twice, k1, rep from * on Needle 2—46 sts.

Rnd 6: * K2, [p2, k2, p1, k2, p2, k1] twice, k1, rep from * on Needle 2.

Rnd 7: * K2, [M1T, p2, k2, p1, k2, p2, M1A, k1] twice, k1, rep from * on Needle 2—54 sts.

Rnd 8: * [K3, p2, k2, p1, k2, p2] twice, k3, rep from * on Needle 2.

Rnd 9: * K2, M1T, k1, p2, C5b, p2, k1, M1A, k1, M1T, k1, p2, C5f, p2, k1, M1A, k2, rep from * on Needle 2—62 sts.

Rnd 10: * K2, [k2, p2, k2, p1, k2, p2, k2, k1] twice, k1, rep from * on Needle 2.

Rnd 11: * K2, [M1T, k2, p2, k2, p1, k2, p2, k2, M1A, k1] twice, k1, rep from * on Needle 2.—70 sts.

Rnd 12: * K5, p2, k2, p1, k2, p2, k7, p2, k2, p1, k2, p2, k5, rep from * on Needle 2.

Rnd 13: * K2, M1T, k3, p2, C5b, p2, k3, M1A, k1, M1T, k3, p2, C5f, p2, k3, M1A, k2, rep from * on Needle 2—78 sts.

Rnd 14: * K2, [p1, k3, p2, k2, p1, k2, p2, k3, p1, k1] twice, k1, rep from * on Needle 2.

Rnd 15: * K2, [M1T, p1, k3, p2, k2, p1, k2, p2, k3, p1, M1A, k1] twice, k1, rep from * on Needle 2—86 sts.

Rnd 16: * K2, [p2, k3, p2, k2, p1, k2, p2, k3, p2, k1] twice, k1, rep from * on Needle 2.

Rnd 17: * K2, M1T, p2, C3b, p2, k2, p1, k2, p2, C3b, p2, M1A, k1, M1T, p2, C3f, p2, k2, p1, k2, p2, C3f, p2, M1A, k1, rep from * on Needle 2—94 sts.

Rnd 18: * K2, [k1, p2, k3, p2, k2, p1, k2, p2, k3, p2, k2] twice, k1, rep from * on Needle 2.

Rnd 19: * K2, [M1T, k1, p2, k3, p2, k2, p1, k2, p2, k3, p2, k1, M1A, k1] twice, k1, rep from * on Needle 2—102 sts.

Rnd 20: * K2, [k2, p2, k3, p2, k2, p1, k2, p2, k3, p2, k3] twice, k1, rep from * on Needle 2.

Rnd 21: * K2, M1T, k2, p2, k3, p2, C5b, p2, k3, p2, k2, M1A, k1, M1T, k2, p2, k3, p2, C5f, p2, k3, p2, k2. M1A, k2, rep from * on Needle 2—110 sts.

Top: Cabled Netbook Cozy, Version 1; Lower: Cabled Netbook Cozy, Version 2
Also shown: Branches, page 162

Cabled Netbook Cozy

Cabled Netbook Cozy, Version 1

Rnd 22: * K2, [p1, k2, p2, k3, p2, k2, p1, k2, p2, k3, p2, k2, p1, k1] twice, k1, rep from * on Needle 2.

Rnd 23: * K2, M1T, [p1, k2, p2, C3b, p2, k2] twice, p1, M1A, k1, M1T, [p1, k2, p2, C3f, p2, k2] twice, p1, M1A, k2, rep from * on Needle 2—118 sts.

Rnd 24: * K3, [p1, k2, p2, k3, p2, k2, p1, k2, p2, k3, p2, k2, p1, k3] twice, rep from * on Needle 2.

Rnd 25: * K2, K2, M1T, k1, p1, k2, p2, k3, p2, C5b, p2, k3, p2, k2, p1, k1, M1A, k1, M1T, k1, p1, k2, p2, k3, p2, C5f, p2, k3, p2, k2, p1, k1, M1A, k2, rep from * on Needle 2—126 sts.

Rnd 26: * [K4, p1, k2, p2, k3, p2, k2, p1, k2, p2, k3, p2, k2, p1, k1] twice, k3, rep from * on Needle 2.

Rnd 27: * K2, M1T, [k2, p1, k2, p2, k3, p2] twice, C5b, M1A, k1, M1T, C5f, [p2, k3, p2, k2, p1, k2] twice, M1A, k2, rep from * on Needle 2—134 sts.

Rnd 28: * K5, p1, [k2, p2, k3, p2, k2, p1] twice, k2, p1, k1, p1, k2, [p1, k2, p2, k3, p2, k2] twice, p1, k5, rep from * on Needle 2.

Measure against netbook for length. The gusset should be about the same length as the hinge side of the netbook.

If more length is needed, work increase rounds as above, working new sts according to the patt as est and working cables as above.

Beg side shaping

Note: St count remains constant until last 2 rnds.

If you needed to add extra length above, use these side shaping instructions as a guide to dec 4 sts on each odd-numbered rnd: K1, ssk, work in patt to just before center st, M1A, k center st, M1T, work in patt to last 3 sts on needle, k2tog, k1. Cont working from Charts A and B, or follow instructions below.

Written Instructions

Rnd 29: * K1, ssk, [k2, p1, k2, p2, C3f, p2, k2, p1] twice, M1A, k1, M1T, [p1, k2, p1, k2, p2, C3b, p2, k2] twice, k2tog, k1, rep from * on Needle 2.

Rnd 30: * K4, p1, [k2, p2, k3, p2, k2, p1] twice, k2, p2, k1, p2, k2, [p1, k2, p2, k3, p2, k2] twice, p1, k4, rep from * on Needle 2.

Rnd 31: * K1, ssk, k1, p1, k2, p2, k3, p2, k2, p1, k2, p2, k3, p2, C5f, p2, M1A, k1, M1T, p2, C5b, p2, k3, p2, k2, p1, k2, p2, k3, p2, k2, p1, k1, k2tog, k1, rep from * on Needle 2.

Rnd 32: * K3, p1, k2, p2, [k3, p2, k2, p1, k2, p2, k3, p2, k2, p1, k2, p2] twice, k3, p2, k2, p1, k3, rep from * on Needle 2.

Rnd 33: * K1, ssk, p1, k2, p2, k3, p2, C5b, p2, k3, p2, k2, p1, k2, p2, k1, M1A, k1, M1T, k1, p2, k2, p1, k2, p2, k3, p2, C5f, p2, k3, p2, k2, p1, k2tog, k1, rep from * on Needle 2.

Rnd 34: * [K2, p1, k2, p2, k3, p2] twice, k2, p1, k2, p2, k5, [p2, k2, p1, k2, p2,

Cabled Netbook Cozy

k3] twice, p2, k2, p1, k2, rep from * on Needle 2.

Rnd 35: * K1, ssk, [k2, p2, C3b, p2, k2, p1] twice, k2, p2, k2, M1A, k1, M1T, k2, p2, k2, [p1, k2, p2, C3f, p2, k2] twice, k2tog, k1, rep from * on Needle 2.

Rnd 36: * K4, [p2, k3, p2, k2, p1, k2] twice, p2, k7, [p2, k2, p1, k2, p2, k3] twice, p2, k4, rep from * on Needle 2.

Measure against netbook for width. The center sts on front and back should reach to the opening edge of the netbook when stretched slightly (tug more than slightly if you are working with wool, or your swatch grew a bit after blocking).

If width is correct, work Rnds 37 and 38 as follows, adding 2 extra sts on each side of center st. Note: to avoid holes, combine methods of M1 increases (i.e., make the first inc using the backwards-loop method, and the second inc using a lifted increase).

Rnd 37: * K1, ssk, k1, p2, k3, p2, C5b, p2, k3, p2, k2, p1, k2, p2, k3, M1A, M1L, k1, M1R, M1T, k3, p2, k2, p1, k2, p2, k3, p2, C5f, p2, k3, p2, k1, k2tog, k1, rep from * on Needle 2—138 sts.

Rnd 38: * K2, [p2, k3, p2, k2, p1, k2] twice, p2, [k3, p1] twice, [k3, p2, k2, p1, k2, p2] twice, k3, p2, k3, rep from * on Needle 2.

If more width is needed, continue working in patt as est, adding sts to each side of center st and decreasing at gusset sides until center st reaches the opening edge of the netbook when stretched slightly. Work new sts according to the patt as est and work cables as above. When width is correct, use instructions above as a guide for last inc rnd, adding 2 extra sts on each side of center st, then work one rnd even in patt.

Complete gusset and corner shaping

Break yarn.

Redistribute sts as follows: transfer first 32 sts on Needle 1 to Needle 2, put center 5 sts from Needle 1 on waste yarn, transfer last 32 sts on Needle 2 to Needle 1, put center 5 sts from Needle 2 on waste yarn. Each needle should have 64 sts. You will now be working back and forth in rows on only one needle at a time.

Work from Chart C on page 155 or written instructions below.

Written Instructions

Row 1 (RS): K1, ssk, p2, C5b, p2, k3, p2, k2, p1, k2, p2, k3, p2, k2tog, k2, ssk, p2, k3, p2, k2, p1, k2, p2, k3, p2, C5f, p2, k2tog, k1—60 sts.

Row 2 (WS): P2, [k2, p2, k1, p2, k2, p3] twice, k2, p4, [k2, p3, k2, p2, k1, p2] twice, k2, p2.

Row 3: K1, ssk, p1, k2, p1, k2, p2, C3b, p2, k2, p1, k2, p2, C3b, p1, k2tog, k2, ssk, p1, C3f, p2, k2, p1, k2, p2, C3f, p2, k2, p1, k2, p1, k2tog, k1—56 sts.

Row 4: P2, k1, p2, k1, p2, k2, p3, k2, p2, k1, p2, k2, p3, k1, p4, k1, p3, k2, p2, k1, p2, k2, p3, k2, p2, k1, p2, k1, p2.

Row 5: K1, ssk, C5b, p2, k3, p2, k2, p1, k2, p2, k3, k2tog, k2, ssk, k3, p2, k2, p1, k2, p2, k3, p2, C5f, k2tog, k1—52 sts.

Row 6: P4, k1, p2, k2, p3, k2, p2, k1, p2, k2, p3, p4, p3, k2, p2, k1, p2, k2, p3, k2, p2, k1, p4.

Row 7: K1, ssk, k1, p1, k2, p2, k3, p2, C5b, p2, k2, k2tog, k2, ssk, k2, p2, C5f, p2, k3, p2, k2, p1, k1, k2tog, k1—48 sts.

Row 8: P3, k1, p2, k2, p3, k2, p2, k1, p2, k2, p8, k2, p2, k1, p2, k2, p3, k2, p2, k1, p3.

Row 9: K1, ssk, p1, k2, p2, C3b, p2, k2, p1, k2, p2, k1, k2tog, k2, ssk, k1, p2, k2, p1, k2, p2, C3f, p2, p1, k2tog, k1—44 sts.

Row 10: P2, k1, p2, k2, p3, k2, p2, k1, p2, k2, p6, k2, p2, k1, p2, k2, p3, k2, p2, k1, p2.

Row 11: K1, ssk, k2, p2, k3, p2, C5b, p2, k2tog, k2, ssk, p2, C5f, p2, k3, p2, k2, k2tog, k1—40 sts.

Row 12: P4, k2, p3, k2, p2, k1, p2, k2, p4, k2, p2, k1, p2, k2, p3, k2, p4,

Row 13: K1, ssk, k1, p2, k3, p2, k2, p1, k2, p1, k2tog, k2, ssk, p1, k2, p1, k2, p2, k3, p2, k1, k2tog, k1—36 sts.

Row 14: [P3, k2] twice, [p2, k1] twice, p4, [k1, p2] twice, [k2, p3] twice.

Row 15: K1, ssk, p2, C3b, p2, k2, p1, k2, k2tog, k2, ssk, k2, p1, k2, p2, C3f, p2, k2tog, k1—32 sts.

Measure for fit. With gentle stretching, the piece should now be able to enclose the netbook entirely on one side. If unsure whether to work additional rows, leave sts

Bags & Cozies Beyond Toes

Cabled Netbook Cozy

on Needle 1, and wait to BO until after working other side.

For a piece that is larger or smaller than the pattern, work the BO row with a double-dec at the beg and end of the needle, as well as a double-dec on each side of the gusset.

Work BO row in pattern as follows, binding off as you go: P1, p3tog, p3, k2, p2, k1, p3tog-tbl, p2, p3tog, k1, p2, k2, p3, p3tog-tbl, p1.

Repeat Rows 1-15, and BO on second side.

Finishing
Attached I-cord trim and loop

With one circular needle and RS facing, starting from either LH corner of gusset, pick up and knit 3 sts for every 4 rows around the opening until you reach the top edge; pick up and knit 1 st for every row across the top edge until you reach the 5 center sts; carefully remove waste yarn and place resulting live sts on LH needle, k5, then cont picking up and knitting sts across top edge and around corners as before until you are back to where you started.

Without breaking yarn, CO 3 sts on LH needle using a cable cast-on. Work applied I-cord as follows: *k2, ssk, transfer sts back to LH needle; repeat from * until all sts have been worked, then work an additional 2.5 inches of I-cord for loop. BO, leaving a long tail. Using a tapestry needle, thread the long tail through the cast-on sts to form a loop, and sew down securely. Weave in all ends.

Install zipper

Turn piece to WS and open zipper. Working on one side of zipper at a time, line up center of zipper with center st and pin to underside of top opening so that zipper teeth are just below edge of I-cord, taking care that zipper pull is to the outside. Next, pin ends of zipper to tops of gusset. Pin rest of edge to zipper, easing fabric evenly.

Using matching thread and sewing needle, sew zipper neatly to underside of top opening. Rep for other side of zipper.

Block zipped, using foil-covered cardboard form.

Note: Do not place damp cozy on netbook, as moisture may harm electronics.

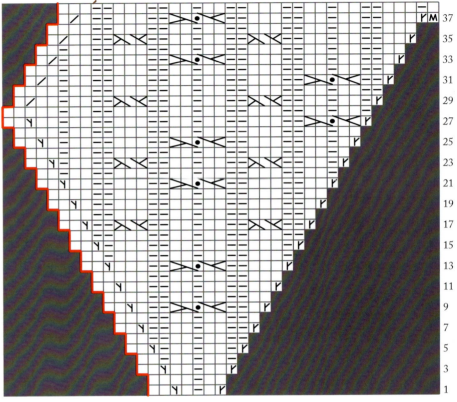

Netbook Cozy Chart B

Cabled Netbook Cozy

Netbook Cozy Chart A

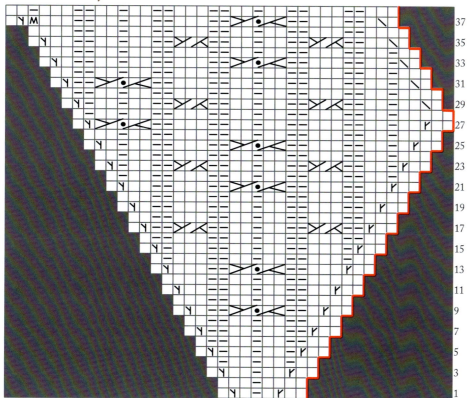

- ☐ Knit
- ⊟ Purl
- ◪ K2tog
- ◩ SSK
- M1A
- M2T
- ▭ Pattern Repeat
- ■ No stitch
- C3f
- C3b
- C5f
- C5b

155

Netbook Cozy Chart C

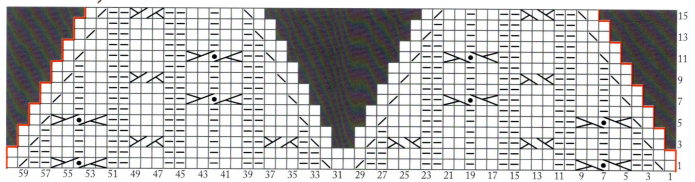

Bags & Cozies ⚓ Beyond Toes

FlatPack

Perhaps the only thing as nice as a great knitting project is a great bag to keep it in, especially one you can wear on your back to keep your hands free for knitting, or yarn shopping. This clever backpack features two drawstring cords, which pull the top of the pack shut when you pull it on your shoulders. Linen Stitch is a simple, two-stitch, two-row slip-stitch pattern that makes a firm fabric, ideal for bags.

Karen Alfke

Flat Pack

Sizes
Smaller (Bigger)

Finished Measurements
Width: 9 (12) inches
Length: 13 (16) inches

Yarn

Version 1 (page 156, left):

[MC} (Solid) Zitron Samoa [100% cotton; [115 yd/105 m per 50 g]; color 27; 2 skeins

[CC] (Variegated) Zitron Samoa Color [100% cotton; 115 yd/105 m per 50 g]; color 122; 2 skeins

Version 2 (page 156, right):

[MC] (Solid) Zitron Samoa [100% cotton; [115 yd/105 m per 50 g]; color 27; 2 skeins

[CC] (Variegated) Zitron Samoa Color [100% cotton; 115 yd/105 m per 50 g]; color 134; 2 skeins

Version 3 (page 156, center):

[MC]: Cascade Cotton Rich DK [64% cotton, 36% nylon; 136 yd/124 m per 50 g]; color 8176 (White); 3 skeins

[CC]: Cascade Cotton Rich DK [64% cotton, 36% nylon; 136 yd/124 m per 50 g]; color 5556 (Turquoise); 3 skeins

Version 4 (shown on cover)

[MC]: Cascade Cotton Rich DK [64% cotton, 36% nylon; 136 yd/124 m per 50 g]; color 7364 (Brown); 3 skeins

[CC]: Cascade Cotton Rich DK [64% cotton, 36% nylon; 136 yd/124 m per 50 g]; color 5606 (Green); 3 skeins

Needles
1 set US #4 [3.5 mm] double-point needles or size to obtain gauge (for I-cord straps)

1 US #8 [5 mm] 16-inch (24-inch) circular needle

1 US #8 [5 mm] needle of any length (for working first few inches of bag in the round)

Notions
Two 24-inch pieces of smooth, fine waste yarn
Two 3/8 inch/9 mm diameter grommets

Gauge
27 sts/44 rows = 4 inches in Linen st [chart] on larger needles

Substitutions
Any DK-weight plant-fiber blend yarn, in 2 solid colors or one solid and one variegated colorway.

Linen Stitch Pattern

In the round, over an odd # of sts:

Rnd 1: *Sl 1 wyif, k1; rep from * to last st, sl 1 wyif

Rnd 2: *K1, sl 1 wyif; rep to last st, k1

Worked flat, over an even # of sts, with slipped selvage sts:

Row 1 (WS): K1-tbl, *sl 1 wyib, p1; rep from * to last st, sl 1 wyib

Row 2 (RS): K1-tbl, *sl 1 wyif, k1; rep to last st, sl 1 wyif

Pattern Notes

The JMCO center bottom rows may appear looser because the linen stitch fabric above it pulls tight. This allows the bag to fold easily along the center line (and allows the center line to be easily identified for measuring); should this looser appearance not be to your liking, you may cast onto two circular needles three sizes smaller than the needles you are using for the body of the bag.

The first few rounds of work will be a bit tight at the corners (where you change needles); be sure to pull the first stitch on the new needle tight to pull the previous needle snug. After the first few rounds, you will be working up the sides of the bag, where it's not necessary to monitor the needle joins quite as closely.

Where a needle ends with a sl 1, drape working yarn behind needles so you maintain the slip strand across the face of that last st.

You will be changing colors every 2 rounds or rows. When picking up a new color to use in the next round, give a gentle tug to take up any slack, but don't pull so tight that the work puckers.

Instructions
See Linen Stitch pattern instructions to the left.

Bag Bottom
With MC and two circular needles, JMCO 60 (80) sts on the bottom needle

and 61 (81) sts on the top needle—121 (161) sts total.

Work Foundation Round as follows:

Needle 1: *K1, sl 1 wyif, rep from * to end of needle.

Needle 2: * K1-tbl, sl 1 tbl wyif, rep from * to last st, end k1-tbl.

Rnd 1-2: Do not cut MC. Join in CC and work 2 rnds Linen Stitch in the round, beg with a Rnd 1.

(Note that on Rnd 2 you are slipping all the sts that are already in CC, and knitting all the sts that are still in MC. At the end of Rnd 2, you thus end up with all sts in CC.)

Rnd 3–4: Lift MC up the inside of the work, give a gentle tug to snug it up, and rep [Rnds 1 and 2] with MC.

Rep [Rnds 1–4] as set (2 rnds of CC and 2 rnds of MC in Linen Stitch), until work measures 1 inch/2.5 cm from JMCO center bottom.

Eyelet Openings for Grommets

Needle 1: Work 6 sts in Linen Stitch, yo, k2tog, resume Linen Stitch, beginning with a sl 1 wyif, until you have 8 sts rem on this needle; yo, k2tog, resume Linen Stitch, beginning with a sl 1 wyif, to end of needle.

Rep on Needle 2. [Stitch count has not changed.

In the next rnd, work the yo's as stitches to stay in pattern.

Bag Body

Resume Linen Stitch in the round, working 2 rnds each of MC and CC, as above. When work measures 3 inches/7.5 cm, you should be far enough away from the JMCO center bottom to work comfortably in the round on one circular needle (for smaller pack, use a 16-inch needle; for larger pack, a 24-inch needle).

Pm for BOR (where you change colors).

Work even in Linen Stitch until work measures 12 inches (15 inches) from JMCO center bottom and you are ready for a Rnd 2 (i.e. the second rnd with CC).

Last rnd: With CC, work 60 (80) sts in patt, pm for halfway point, work to last 3 sts of rnd.

Cord Casings

Beginning at 3 sts before end of round, and with CC, k2tog and then BO next 2 sts (knitwise), removing BOR marker as you come to it.

Cut CC, leaving a 24-inch tail. Lift up MC, and beg with sl 1 wyif and MC, work in Linen Stitch to 1 st before halfway marker. BO next 2 sts (knitwise), removing halfway marker as you come to it—58 (78) sts on each needle.

With MC and beg with sl 1 wyif, work in Linen Stitch to bound-off gap at end of rnd; end wyif and slip last st.

Cord casings will be worked separately back and forth.

Flat Pack, Version 2

With MC, work a WS row of Linen Stitch worked flat (see instructions on page 158). Join a new strand of CC, leaving a 24-inch tail, and work 2 rows Linen Stitch flat using CC. Continue working Linen Stitch, rep 2 rows of MC followed by 2 rows of CC, until casing measures 2 inches from the bound-off sts and you are ready for a WS row in MC.

Next row (WS): BO with MC, purling all sts firmly and evenly.

Cut both MC and CC, leaving 6-inch tails; weave in tails on WS of flap.

Flat Pack

For second cord casing: With WS facing and using remaining live sts and a new strand of MC, work a WS row of Linen Stitch as est.

Join in a new strand of CC and work a RS row and a WS row. Continue as for first casing. When same height as first casing, BO and weave in tails.

Cord Straps (Make 2)

With MC or CC (whichever you prefer), cast on 4 sts onto smaller-sized double-pointed needle.

Work I-cord as follows: *K1-tbl, k3; do not turn—slide sts to opposite end of the needle, rep from * until strap measures 60 inches. BO all 4 sts.

Weave in ends by threading end onto a darning needle and stuffing it up into the cord.

Note: Straps may stretch a few inches with wear, but length can be readjusted later by adjusting the knots.

Finishing

Choose which face of bag you want facing out as worn. (Grommets may have a WS and a RS as applied.)

With front of bag facing up, ease stem of male grommet piece down through yarn over holes of both layers of fabric at one corner. Turn bag over and center female grommet piece over stem; using grommet tool and a hammer, bang grommet pieces together, sandwiching both layers of fabric together inside the grommet.

Repeat at opposite corner (remembering to flip bag over to begin with front of bag facing).

Step 1: Lay both straps along the WS face of cord casing on one side of bag, then fold casing over cords and sew bound-off edge of casing to a row of sts level with the bound-off sides.

Cord casing will thus measure 1 inch tall when folded in half and sewn down. Use a light whip-stitch, and do not pull sewing yarn so tight that you pucker the seam.

Step 2: Take one end of one of one cord and fold it to make a U-turn at this side; lay it along the WS face of the opposite casing. Starting at the opposite side of the bag, take the OTHER cord and fold it to make a U-turn coming the other way. Fold casing down over these and sew down as for other side.

Step 3: Feed ends of cords up through the grommet on the same side of the bag, and knot together, close to the cord ends. Cord straps will thus gather the top of the bag when pulled.

Step 1

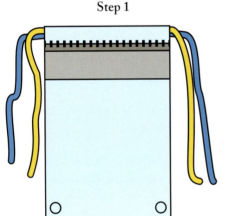

Step 2

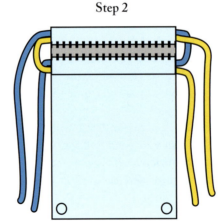

Step 3

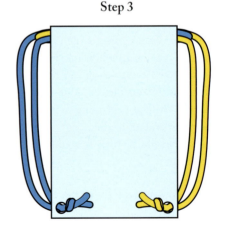

162

Branches & Round-Up

I have always been inspired by fall colors, the green that surrounds me here in Oregon and the symmetry of the old Pendleton blankets.

The stripes of Round-Up remind me of evening rodeos, the green of Oregon and the sunsets and scrub brush of my childhood in Texas.

The luxurious, light airiness of Oregon snow on twisting dark branches inspired Branches.

Leslie Cumming

Branches & Round-Up

Finished Measurements
14 inches x 14 inches

Yarn
For Round-Up, Version 1:
ShiBui Yarns Merino Worsted [100% superwash merino wool; 191 yd/175 m per 100 g skein]
[MC] color: Pagoda; 1 skein
[CC1] color: Bark, 1 skein
[CC2] color: Ivory; 1 skein
[CC3] color: Wasabi; 1 skein

For Round-Up, Version 2 (page 162, bottom):
[MC] Cascade Yarns Pure Alpaca [100% baby alpaca; 220 yd/200 m per 3.5 oz/100 g skein]; color: #3007; 1 skein
[CC1] Cascade Yarns Eco Alpaca [100% pure undyed alpaca; 220 yd/200 m per 3.5 oz/100 g skein]; color: #1515, 1 skein
[CC2] Cascade Yarns Eco Alpaca [100% pure undyed alpaca; 220 yd/200 m per 3.5 oz/100 g skein]; color: #1510; 1 skein
[CC3] Cascade Yarns Pure Alpaca [100% baby alpaca; 220 yd/200 m per 3.5 oz/100 g skein]; color: #3029; 1 skein

For Branches (page 162, top):
Cascade Yarns Pure Alpaca [100% baby alpaca; 220 yd/200 m per 3.5 oz/100 g skein]; color: #3013; 2 skeins

Needles
2 US #6 [4.0 mm] 24-inch circular needles or size needed to obtain gauge

Notions
Stitch markers
Tapestry needle
Four 1-inch buttons
Sewing needle
14-inch to 16-inch pillow form (pillows are shown on 16-inch forms)

Gauge
20 sts/28 rows = 4 inches in St st

Substitutions
Any wool, alpaca, cashmere or combination that allows the knitter to achieve gauge.

Pattern Note
C4b (Cable 4 back): Sl next 2 st to cable needle and hold in back, k next 2 st, k sts from cable needle.

Instructions
Both pillows:
Using Judy's Magic Cast-On and circular needles, cast on 70 st to each needle—140 stitches total.
Begin working in the round.

Round-Up only:
Knit around for 13 inches in the following stripe patt:
12 rnds of MC.
3 rnds of CC1.
2 rnds of CC2.
5 rnds of CC3.
3 rnds of CC1.
3 rnds of MC.
5 rnds of CC3.
3 rnds or CC1.
2 rnds of CC2.
4 rnds of CC1.
13 rnds of MC.
3 rnds of CC3.
2 rnds of CC2.
3 rnds of CC1.
5 rnds of Cc3.
3 rnds of CC1.
9 rnds of MC.
2 rnds of CC2.
5 rnds of CC3.
3 rnds of CC1.
1 rnd of MC, turn work.

The back and the front will now be worked separately in rows in MC only.

Branches only:
Work either written instructions or chart of Branches Cable Pattern on page 165.

Rnd 1: K29, pm, work 26 sts in Cable Pattern, pm, k85.
Rnd 2: K29, sm, work next rnd of cable pattern, sm, k85.

Rep [Rnd 2] until pillow measures 13 inches. Turn work.

The back and the front will now be worked separately in rows.

Both Pillows:
Back:
Starting with WS facing, work the following 5 rows:
Row 1: P70.
Row 2: K70.

Beyond Toes ⚓ Comfy Things

Branches & Round-Up

Row 3–5: K70.
BO back.

Front:
Starting with RS facing, attach MC and work 15 rows for the pillow flap as follows:
Row 1: K70.
Row 2: P70.
Rows 3–8: Rep [Rows 1–2].

Make buttonholes:
Row 9: K13, [BO 2, k12] 4 times, k1.
Row 10: P13, [CO 2, p12] 4 times, p1.

Rows 11–14: Rep [Rows 1–2].
Rows 15–18: K70.
BO front.

Finishing
Weave in ends.
Lightly dampen with spray bottle and block to measurements.

Place front flap overlapping back by approximately 2 inches and mark button placement. Sew buttons in place on back flap.

Top: Branches
Center: Round-Up, Version 2
Bottom: Round-Up, Version 1

Branches Cable Pattern
Rnd 1–2: [p1, k4], 5 times, p1.
Rnd 3: [p1, c4b, p1, k4], 2 times, p1, c4b, p1.
Rnd 4–10: [p1, k4], 5 times, p1.
Rnd 11: [p1, k4, p1, c4b], 2 times, p1, k4, p1.
Rnd 12–14: [p1, k4], 5 times, p1.
Rnd 15: [p1, k4, p1, c4b], 2 times, p1, k4, p1.
Rnd 16–22: [p1, k4], 5 times, p1.
Rnd 23: [p1, c4b, p1, k4], 2 times, p1, c4b, p1.
Rnd 24: [p1, k4], 5 times, p1.

Branches Cable Chart

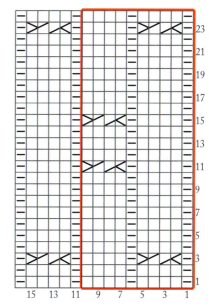

- ☐ Knit
- ⊟ Purl
- ⊠ C4b
- ▢ Pattern repeat

166

Pippa

The design for Pippa the Pig grew from a simple variation on Judy's Magic Cast-On that I use when knitting top-down caps for the newborns at my local hospital. I shared it with Judy, we decided it looked like a pig's tail, and a challenge was issued: design a pattern for a stuffed pig, worked from the tush end up. What a humble beginning for a glorious creature!

Deb Barnhill

Pippa

Finished Measurements
Approximately 10 inches long and 7 inches tall.

Yarn
Version 1 (page 166):
Cascade 220 [100% wool; 220 yd/200 m per 100 g skein]; color: 4192; 1 skein
Version 2 (this page):
Dream In Color Classy [100% superfine Australian merino superwash wool; 250 yd per 4 oz skein]; color: Petal Shower; 1 skein

Needles
2 US #5 [3.75 mm] 24-inch circular needles

Notions
6 stitch markers, one in contrast to others
Darning needle
Polyester fiberfill for stuffing
Two 18 mm eyes with washer backs
Small amount scrap yarn for detailing (optional)

Gauge
24 sts/32 rows = 4 inches in St st
Gauge is not critical and will change after stuffing. Fabric should be tight enough to keep stuffing from showing through.

Substitutions
Any worsted weight yarn, worked at tighter gauge than stated on the ball band.

Pattern Notes
This pattern is written to be worked on 2 circular needles. The Magic Loop method or double-pointed needles may be substituted.

To work the entire pig from a single skein without extra yarn ends to weave in, wind the skein into a center-pull ball and work the pig to the body from the inside end of the ball. Work the legs from the outside end of the ball, and then return to the body. In place of this, you may break the yarn, work the legs, and then rejoin the end to complete to body and front end.

Instructions

Tail
Using Judy's Magic Cast-On, CO 3 sts to each needle—6 sts total. Following instructions for "Twisted I-Cord Circular Cast-On—I-Cord Island" on page 18, knit until I-cord is 4 inches long. Twist I-cord 6 full rotations.

Place BOR marker and knit 1 rnd.

Note: after this step, there may be a small hole at the join. See Finishing on page 170 for how to remedy this.

Rear End
Rnd 1: [K1, m1, pm] 5 times, k1, m1, sl BOR marker—12 sts.
Rnd 2: [K to marker, m1, sm] 6 times—18 sts. Rep Rnd 2 [every rnd] 3 times, then [every other rnd] 9 times, ending with an inc rnd—90 sts after completing Rnd 23.

Next Rnd: Knit around, removing first, 2nd, 4th, and 5th markers—3rd marker rems as side marker.

Work in St st until work from base of tail measures approximately 4.5 inches.

Pippa, Version 2

Pippa

Mark Rear Legs:

Rnd 1: K to side marker, sm, k8, p10, k9, p10, k to end of rnd.

Rnds 2 – 4: K to side marker, sm, [k8, p1] twice, k9, p1, k8, p1, k to end of rnd.

Rnd 5: Rep Rnd 1.

Work in St st for 2 inches more.

Mark Front Legs:

Work Rnds 1–5 as for Rear Legs.

Right Ear

Set-up rows: K16, w&t. P10, w&t.

Rows 1, 3, 5, 7, 9 (RS): K to 1 st before wrapped st, w&t.

Rows 2, 4, 6, 8 (WS): P to 1 st before wrapped st, w&t.

Row 10: P1, w&t.

Row 11: K1, k next st tog with its wrap, w&t.

Even Rows 12–18 (WS): P to double-wapped st, p it tog with its wraps, w&t.

Odd Rows 13–19 (RS): K to double-wrapped st, k it tog with its wraps, w&t.

Row 20 (WS): P to double wrapped st, p it tog with its wraps, do not wrap, turn.

Row 21 (RS): Sl 1p, k to double wrapped st, k it tog with its wraps.

Left Ear

Setup Rows: K22, w&t. P10, w&t.

Work rows 1-21 as for right ear. K to end of rnd.

Left: Pippa, Version 1; right: Pippa, Version 2

Shape forehead

Rnd 1: K4, k2tog, k10, pm, ssk, k9, k2tog, pm, k10, ssk, k to end of rnd—86 sts.

Rnd 2: K to marker, sm, ssk, k to 2 sts before marker, k2tog, sm, k to end of rnd—2 sts dec.

Rnds 3–5: Rep [Rnd 2] and on Rnd 5, remove all markers; after ending Rnd 5, k5 and pm for new BOR marker—78 sts.

Legs

Place body sts on hold while working legs from opposite end of skein.

Pick up and k 30 sts around the perimeter of a marked back-leg rectangle: 10 sts along each long edge and 5 sts along each short edge. Do this on the very outside of the rectangle; no purl sts should show. Pm for BOR.

Work in St st for approximately 1 inch.

Next rnd: [K5, pm] 5 times, k to end of rnd.

Dec Rnds 1–4: [K to 2 sts before marker, k2tog, sm] 6 times and on Rnd 4, remove all marker—6 sts rem.

Cut yarn, leaving a 6-inch tail.

Stuff leg very firmly. Using a darning needle, draw yarn through rem 6 sts and pull to tighten. Insert yarn straight down through the center of the leg and bring

Pippa

Pippa, Version 1

yarn end through to inside of pig. Secure tightly; this should create a bit of a "pucker" on the bottom surface of the leg.

Repeat for each of the legs.

Resume work from first end of skein for remainder of piece.

Shape Face

Set-up rnd: [K13, pm] 5 times, k to end of rnd.

Dec rnd: [K to 2 sts before marker, k2tog, sm] 6 times—72 sts.

Cont in St st and rep Dec rnd [every other rnd] 3 times, then [every rnd] 5 times—24 sts.

Apply eyes, using photo as a guide. Stuff pig to the head, being sure to fill short-row ears to make them stand up.

Snout

Work in St st until work from base of snout measures about 1.25 inches, then proceed with shaping as follows:

Set-up rnd: [K4, pm] 5 times, k to end of rnd.

Rnds 1–2: [K to 2 sts before marker, k2tog, sm], 6 times—12 sts at end of Rnd 2.
Rnd 3: Removing markers, k2tog around—6 sts.

Cut yarn, leaving a 6-inch tail.

Stuff remainder of pig, being sure to stuff snout firmly.

Using a darning needle, draw yarn through rem 6 sts and pull to tighten. Insert yarn straight down through the center of the snout and bring yarn end through to inside of pig. Secure tightly to create a bit of a pucker on the snout's base.

Finishing

Use the tail from the CO to cinch up the small gap at the tail end, burying end inside pig. Bury any remaining ends inside pig.

Use contrasting-colored yarn to duplicate stitch mouth, detailing as in photo if desired, bringing ends to the inside of pig.

Pippa, Version 2

References

Abbreviations & Symbols

Abbreviation	Meaning
*	Repeat instructions as directed.
[ ]	Repeat instructions inside the brackets as directed.
2/1 LC	Slip next 2 stitches to cable needle and hold to front, knit 1 stitch, knit 2 stitches from cable needle.
2/1 RC	Slip next stitch to cable needle and hold to back, knit 2 stitches, knit stitche from cable needle.
2/1 LPC	Slip next 2 stitches to cable needle and hold to front, purl 1 stitch, knit 2 stitches from cable needle.
2/1 RPC	Slip next stitch to cable needle and hold to back, knit 2 stitches; purl 1 stitch from cable needle.
11/1/11 cable	Slip next 12 stitches onto cable needle and hold to front, work next 11 stitches as directed by pattern, slip left-most stitch from cable needle back onto the left needle, knit this stitch, work remaining 10 stitches from cable needle as directed by pattern.
alt	Alternate
B	Place bead
B6	The 6 border stitches on Monica's Seamen's Scarf
beg	Begin/beginning
bet	Between
BO	Bind off
BOR	Beginning of round
C3b	Slip next 2 stitches to cable needle and hold in back, knit next stitch, knit 2 stitches from cable needle.
C3f	Slip 1 next stitch to cable needle and hold in front, knit next 2 stitches, knit stitch from cable needle.
C4b	Slip next 2 stitches to cable needle and hold in back, knit next 2 stitches, knit 2 stitches from cable needle.
C4f	Slip next 2 stitches to cable needle and hold in front, knit next 2 stitches, knit 2 stitches from cable needle.
C5b	Slip next 3 stitches to cable needle and hold in back, knit next 2 stitches, slip purl stitch from cable needle back to left needle and purl, knit 2 stitches from cable needle.
C5f	Slip next 3 stitches to cable needle and hold in front, knit next 2 stitches, slip purl stitch from cable needle back to left needle and purl, knit 2 stitches from cable needle.
CC	Contrasting color
cdd	Centered Double Decrease: slip two stitches together knitwise, knit next stitch, pass the slipped stitches over the knit stitch.
cdi	Centered Double Increase: Knit the next stitch through the back loop and then through the front loop. Insert left needle from left to right under vertical strand between stitches just made; knit this strand through the back loop.
cm	Centimeter(s)
cn	Cable needle
CO	Cast on
cont.	Continue

Abbreviations & Symbols

Abbreviation	Meaning
dec	Decrease/decreases/decreasing
dpn	Double pointed needle(s)
EOR	End of round
est	Established
g	Gram
inc	Increase/increases/increasing
JMCO	Judy's Magic Cast-On
JSSBO	Jeny's Surprisingly Stretchy Bind Off, first published in Knitty.com, Fall 2009 (http://www.knitty.com). [4]
k	Knit
k2tog	Knit 2 stitches together
k3tog	Knit 3 stitches together
k3tog tbl	Knit 3 stitches together through their back loops
kfb	Knit into front of stitch, then knit into the back of the same stitch.
KRL	Knit Right Loop: insert the right needle into right loop of stitch just below next stitch on the left needle; place the loop onto left needle and knit it.
KLL	Knit Left Loop: insert the left needle into the left loop of stitch two rows below the last completed stitch on the right needle; knit this stitch through the back loop.
kwise	Knitwise
LDC	Left Dropped Cable: drop next stitch to front. Knit next 2 stitches. Return dropped stitch to left needle and knit it.
LH	Left hand
{loop}	Indicates position of circular needle loops to enable Magic Loop knitting.
m	Meter(s)
M1	Make one stitch
M1A	Make 1, away: make a backwards loop on the right needle with the working yarn exiting the back of the loop.
M1L	Make 1, left-leaning: from the front, lift loop between stitches with left needle, knit into back of loop.
M1P	Make one purl stitch.
M1R	Make 1, right-leaning: from the back, lift loop between stitches with left needle, knit into front loop.
M1T	Make 1, towards: make a backwards loop on the right needle with the working yarn exiting the front of the loop.
MC	Main color
mm	Millimeter(s)
oz	Ounce(s)
p	Purl
p2tog	Purl 2 stitches together
p3tog	Purl 3 stitches together
p2tog tbl	Purl 2 stitches together through their back loops
patt	Pattern(s)
pfb	Purl into front of stitch, then purl into the back of the same stitch.
pm	Place marker
prev	Previous
psso	Pass slipped stitch over
pwise	Purlwise
RDC	Right Dropped Cable: Slip next 2 stitches. Drop next stitch to front. Return slipped stitches to left needle. Return dropped stitch to left needle. Knit these 3 stitches.
rem	Remain/remaining

References — Beyond Toes

Abbreviations & Symbols

Abbreviation	Meaning
rep	Repeat(s)
rev st st	Reverse stockinette stitch
RH	Right hand
RLCinc	Right-leaning cable increase: k into the fronts of the next 2 stitches, without dropping those stitches from the left needle; knit the same 2 stitches from the left needle again, dropping them from the left needle as usual. 2 stitches increased to 4 stitches.
RLCdec	Right-leaning cable decrease: slip next 2 stitches to cable needle and hold at back of work; [knit stitch on left needle together with stitch on cable needle] twice. 4 stitches decreased to 2 stitches.
rnd(s)	Round(s)
RS	Right side
sk	Skip
sk2p	Slip 1 stitch, knit next 2 stitches together, pass slipped stitch over the knit stitch; 2 stitches have been decreased.
skp	Slip 2 stitch, knit next stitch, pass slipped stitch over the knit stitch. 1 stitch decreased.
sl	Slip
sl st	Slip stitch(es)
sl 1	Slip 1:
	With yarn held to wrong side, or
	With yarn held to right side.
sm	Slip marker
ssk	Slip the next two stitches individually knitwise, knit these 2 stitches together through their back loops.
ssp	Slip the next two stitches individually knitwise, then slip the same 2 stitches purlwise back to the left needle. Purl these 2 stitches together through their back loops.
st st	Stockinette stitch
st(s)	Stitch(es)
t2r	Twist two right: cross second stitch in front of first stitch; knit stitch in front, purl stitch in back.
t3b	Twist three back: cross second and third stitches in front over first stitch; knit two stitch in front through their back loops, purl stitch in back.
t3f	Twist three front: cross first and second stitches in front over third stitch; purl stitch in back, knit 2 stitches in front through their back loops.
tbl	Through back loop
tog	Together
w&t	Wrap and turn:
	On a knit row: slip the next stitch purlwise, bring the yarn to the front, and replace the slipped stitch back onto the left needle. Turn the work.
	On a purl row: slip the next stitch purlwise, bring the yarn to the back, and replace the slipped stitch back onto the left needle. Turn the work.
WS	Wrong side
wyib	With yarn in back
wyif	With yarn in front
yd(s)	Yard(s)
yfwd	Yarn forward
yo	Yarn over

About The Designers

Cindy Abernethy

Cindy has been crafting almost since she could walk. Crochet and knitting have always been her primary medium. Most days you can find her sharing her passion for all things fiber at her Portland, Oregon shop, Urban Fiber Arts. Whether she's being "the Sherlock Holmes of knitting" to help a customer solve the mystery of a dropped stitch, or pointing out the "souvenir" section of local products to out-of-town visitors, you're sure to find her smiling whenever fiber is near.

Karen Alfke

Karen's biggest "aha!" moment in knitting came in 1998, when she picked up a knitting magazine at the grocery store and played with a stitch pattern contained therein… Thus was her obsession with Linen Stitch born! More than a decade later, she's still not done playing with the possibilities of this half-woven, half-knitted stitch pattern.

Deb Barnhill

Deb Barnhill happily knits for her husband and two daughters in Nova Scotia. She blogs at www.knittingpharm.com and has designed for Knitty.com, Knotions.com, Alpacas Magazine and several local yarn stores. Deb started her teaching career with a bang, participating in the inaugural Sock Summit in 2009.

Lorilee Beltman

Lorilee, former owner of City Knitting in Grand Rapids, Michigan, now spends more time designing and teaching. She appreciates beautiful yarn, but gets even more excited by wacky knitting maneuvers. She believes the process of knitting can actually make the knitter a better person. Married to an engineer and mom to three teenage boys, her life is devoid of the color pink.

About The Designers

Cat Bordhi

Cat Bordhi is frequently propelled out of bed in the night by the sudden realization of a new knitting technique or design. A former school teacher, she has authored five innovative knitting books and a novel, and teaches Moebius knitting, sock architecture, and creativity techniques all over North America. You can find her knitting tutorials on YouTube.

JC Briar

A self-confessed "technique freak" and "skill junkie," JC dabbles in all kinds of knitting, but has a special fondness for textured knitting and novel construction techniques. If it involves lace, cables, or seamless construction, it's sure to catch her eye. Author of *Charts Made Simple*, she shares her enthusiasm by teaching at shops and fiber festivals, building her students' confidence by expressing concepts clearly and by presenting skills in a digestible progression.

Chris Church

Chris Church has been designing for 3 years, but has been knitting for over 13 years. Her first Christmas in college, a friend's Pakistani grandmother taught her to knit. It so changed her life that she switched from engineering to pursue a degree in Fiber Arts at Oregon College of Art & Craft. Most of her studies focused on Fashion Design. She loves creating unique one-of-a-kind items, but fashion is about multiple copies. She then remembered her doodled knitting designs in the margins of her school work since that fateful lesson that changed her life. She lives in Washington state with her husband, 2 dogs, a rabbit and a little one born in October 2010. Catch up with her on Pursuitoffiber.com.

Leslie Cumming

The owner of Urban Fiber Studio, Leslie's passion for the needlearts, knitting, editing, fashion and design has translated into a career. Leslie works full time and teaches part-time in her local yarn shops. A love of cables, texture and better design principles has led her on a never-ending quest for knowledge of the craft of design and industry. She is currently working with several knitwear designers and organizations in the needlearts industry doing marketing, public relations and editing. She is taking course work to complete the Nihon Vogue Certification Level 2 and has attended The Academy of Arts Knitwear Design program.

Kathleen Fajardo

Kathleen has enjoyed a variety of needlework since being taught by her beloved grandmother to embroider as a child. Crocheting for over twenty years led to knitting and, eventually, the desire to design her own projects. Kathleen resides in the beautiful Pacific Northwest with her husband and children.

Nadine Foster

Nadine Foster was taught to knit as a child. Her hands kept busy over the years, but worked in the confines of traditional knitting patterns. In 2007, she discovered a program called Knitty Gritty on TV. In one episode, Cat Bordhi showed her Coriolis sock and Nadine became infatuated. As she tried out JMCO and toe up construction, Nadine thought "purse." After discovering Elizabeth Zimmermann and Barbara Walker, Nadine's knitting has never been the same and she truly has become an obsessed knitter. Her favorite projects are socks, lace shawls and, of course, bags.

About The Designers

Sivia Harding

Sivia Harding is known for her exceptional beaded knits. Her work can be seen online on Ravelry, Patternfish, Twist Collective, Knitty.com, and her website at www.siviaharding.com. Her published work can be found in many books, print magazines, subscription clubs, and self published patterns. She has been designing professionally since 2003.

Stephen Houghton

Stephen Houghton dreams of Paris from his often-chilly home in San Francisco. Since 2004, he's been a needle junkie online at www.hizknits.com. He's been in your ears with the YKNIT.com podcast, on TV's Knitty Gritty, and in your brain as a teacher at Sock Summit. His designs have been included in the Rockin' Sock Club, Knitting it Old School, and the Knitter's Book of Socks. When he's not slinging pixels at his day job, he trains to be circus freak, travels the globe with his photographer husband Christopher Hall, and snuggles Janie Sparkles and Decibelle Doughnut, their French Bulldogs.

Janel Laidman

Janel Laidman has enjoyed knitting socks ever since she was an exchange student in Denmark where she observed Danish girls knitting socks in class and thought they were the coolest people she knew. She loves to explore different sock construction and was delighted when she discovered Judy's Magic Cast-On. Janel lives, knits and dreams in beautiful Eugene, Oregon where she is always hard at work on her next pattern. She is the author of two sock knitting books; The Enchanted Sole and The Eclectic Sole

Kendra Nitta

Kendra Nitta knits, sews, and designs primarily with plant-based fibers. You can find her work in Interweave Knits Holiday Gifts, Knitcircus, Knitty, and on her blog, www.missknitta.com.

Gayle Roehm

Gayle is a former management consultant who now devotes herself to knitting and other fiber arts. Her designs have appeared in Knitter's Magazine, Interweave Knits and other publications. She lives in Maryland, when she's not indulging her incurable wanderlust.

Samantha Roshak

More than 10 years ago Samantha turned her back on her life in high tech to devote her time and passion to softer things. She's happy at home, surrounded by fiber, family, and furry friends spending her days knitting, spinning, writing, designing, and being thankful she can work in her pajamas. You can read more about her adventures on her blog http://www.knitquest.com or checkout her video patterns and tips at http://fibersidelounge.ning.com.

Joan Schrouder

Joan Schrouder, from Eugene, Oregon, loves teaching knitters to reason out solutions. Intriguing construction details, seamless knitting and ethnic styles fascinate her. She has been teaching classes at national knitting conventions for more than 20 years and travels the country teaching for guilds and yarn shops. In the past she has designed for knitting magazines and yarn companies, and now for special occasions like this one. She also answers technique questions on various internet knitting lists and Ravelry (as "schrouderknits").

About The Designers

Myrna A. I. Stahman

Myrna's self-published book, *Stahman's Shawls and Scarves – Lace Faroese-Shaped Shawls From the Neck Down and Seamen's Scarves*, is a classic in the world of lace knitting. Judy's Magic Cast-On works great for all the Seamen's scarves in *Stahman's Shawls and Scarves*. Myrna's designs have been published in Wild Fibers, Interweave Knits, the Ashford Wheel, Vogue Knitting, Knitter's Magazine and the Storey One-Skein Wonders books. She is currently publishing pattern collections for Buffalo Gold Yarns and continues work on two lace knitting books.

Jeny Staiman

Jeny Staiman is a mom, a usability engineer, and a self-diagnosed knitting geek. For the past 15 years she has knitted primarily socks, hats, and gloves (i.e., short attention span for knitting in straight lines) and has recently been seduced into the world of knitting moebii and other nonorientable mathematical forms.

Duffy Stephens

Duffy Stephens is a life-long resident of Portland Oregon where she finds inspiration in the shapes of the greenery and architecture around her. She has been playing with various forms of fiber since her teens including quilting, needlepoint, and clothing design. Knitting entered her life in 2002 and has remained a constant presence since then though it competes now with handspinning. When she is not busy corralling her stash she is cat mom to three.

Bobbie Wallace

Bobbie learned many needle arts as a child, but knitting continues to be her favorite. She lives near Portland, Oregon where she helped found PDX Knit Bloggers and Portland Spinnerati, is married to ToolMan (who made the beautiful wood shawl pins in this book), and blogs at www.tiggywinkleknits.blogspot.com. Amazingly, she is project monogamous.

References ~ Beyond Toes

Resources

Your Local Yarn Shop

Local yarn shops provide knitters with tools, materials, knowledge, training, and community. They celebrate our successes and commiserate with us when projects don't quite work out as planned. Please support them whenever possible.

Shawl Pins

Plover Designs
Portland, Oregon
http://www.Ploverdesigns.com

Tiggywinkle & Toolman
Hillsboro, Oregon
Available exclusively from Urban Fiber Arts in Portland, Oregon: http://www.urbanfiberarts.com

Beads

Artbeads
Gig Harbor, Washington
http://www.artbeads.com

Earthfaire
http://www.earthfaire.com

Yarn

Abstract Fiber
Portland, Oregon
http://www.abstractfiber.com

Blue Moon Fiber Arts
Scappoose, Oregon
http://www.bluemoonfiberarts.com

Blue Sky Alpacas
Cedar, Minnesota
http://www.blueskyalpacas.com

Brown Sheep
Mitchell, Nebraska
http://www.brownsheep.com

Buffalo Gold
http://www.buffalogold.net

Cascade Yarns
http://www.cascadeyarns.com

Crystal Palace Yarns
Richmond, California
http://www.straw.com

Resources

Curious Creek Fibers
San Diego, California
http://www.curiouscreek.com

Lanaknits Designs Hemp for Knitting
Nelson, British Columbia
http://www.lanaknits.com

Pico Accuardi Dyeworks
Portland, Oregon
http://www.picoaccuardi.com

Shibui Knits
Portland, Oregon
http://www.shibuiknits.com

Skacel Collection
http://www.skacelknitting.com

Stitchjones
http://www.stitchjones.com

References ~ Beyond Toes

Acknowledgements

It does, indeed, take a village to create a book. I am eternally grateful for the help that the following have provided. Needless to say, any errors found within these pages are entirely mine.

- Thank you Vivian from the bottom of my heart! You immediately saw my vision and brought it to life with your beautiful photography.

- Cat, you knew there was a book in there somewhere and poked and teased until it emerged, and then gave it a wonderfully green and energetic environment in which to grow.

- To the Visionaries: I could not have dreamed of a more generous and creative group. I have learned more from you than I could have imagined possible.

- A huge multitude of hugs to all of the wonderful designers who believed that this project would see the light. Thank you for trusting me patiently with your designs.

- To the Thursday night Tangle knitters: JMCO was launched via your gentle boosts. Can you believe what happened next?

- Thanks and hugs to the PDX Knit Bloggers, but especially the Wednesday Night Sip & Stitch gang. You listened when I needed an ear, and told me what I needed to hear—even when it wasn't what I wanted to know. And you kept reminding me that there was this book thing…

- Most grateful thanks to Charlotte Quiggle, for thorough and patient technical editing.

- A big thank you to Dawn Seymour, who not only let us take over her house, but entertained the wee ones with amazing good grace.

- And finally to all of the knitters, near and far, who contacted me just to say thanks: you will never know how much your words meant.

- The following adventurous knitters provided sample and test knitting, without which this would be a much less colorful book:
  Angela M. Aragon-Henslee
  Jen Clodius
  Nadine Foster
  Tracy Irwin
  Veronica Johnson
  Rachel Nichols
  Katrin Silvius
  Farrah Weinert

- The intrepid models alternately froze and sweltered, and yet managed to look like they were having fun:
  Anatole Aubrey
  Adam Becker
  Lorelei Culbertson
  Natassia Haas
  Chris Martin
  Lucy Martin
  Hazel Nichols
  Carla Reppeteaux
  Emiel Schuttloffel

- Interior location was provided by Dawn Seymour, Eric Hall, and their family.

Beyond Toes ~ References

Acknowledgements

Endnotes

1. Reimann, Siiri and Edasi, Aime. *The Haapsalu Shawl: A Knitted Lace Tradition from Estonia.* Saara Publishing House, 2009.

2. "Over The Top Mittens" was first published in *Twists and Turns® The Newsletter for Lovers of Cable Knitting*, in the Winter 2009 issue.

3. Stitch pattern used in November Street was found in: *Collected, corrected and arranged by A.M., Home Work, A Choice Collection of Useful Designs for Crochet and Knitting Needle.* Toronto: Rose Publishing Co., 1891: 355 – 356.

4. "Jeny's Surprisingly Stretchy Bind Off" was first published in Knitty.com, Fall 2009. <http://www.knitty.com>.

Photo credits

All photography except otherwise noted below: © 2011, Vivian Aubrey

Page 9: Unknown. '"The Aunts" visiting Yellowstone—Lake Lodge, July, 1925'. N.d. Photograph. From the collection of the author.

Page 9: Unknown. 'Road Trip near Mackay, ID'. N.d. Photograph. From the collection of the author.

Page 10: Unknown. 'Lechleiter family: Grandpa, Grandma, Aunt Georgianne (on trike), Alice (Mama)'. N.d. Photograph. From the collection of the author.

Page 10: Unknown. 'John & Alice Fanning'. N.d. Photograph. From the collection of the author.

Page 11: Fanning, Alice S. 'Close encounter with a frog. Judy & John (Dads)'. N.d. Photograph. From the collection of the author.

Page 11: Becker, Judy A. 'Adam in Death Valley'. 12/29/2005. Photograph. From the collection of the author.

Port JMCO	**page 14**
Branches & Round-Up	page 162
Cabled Netbook Cozy	page 148
Charlie's Creature Cap	page 41
FlatPack	page 156
Headbumps	page 45
Over The Top Mittens	page 87
Poncho Puzzle	page 137
Swept Off My Feet	page 75
Spring Fever Socks	page 93
Provisional Bay	**page 16**
Blockalicious	page 142
Bobsled Mittens	page 81
Eye Of The Needle	page 63
Haberdasher	page 31
Laurel Jane's Cap	page 25
Mokosh	page 127
Magic Cowl & Wristlet	page 55
Monica's Seamen's Scarf	page 69
November Street	page 120
Pasarela	page 115
Tubular Reef	**page 17**
Djinn	page 107
1-Cord Island	**page 18**
Pippa	page 166
Magic Bridge	**page 20**
Three-Point Socks	page 99
Double Straits	**page 22**
Leaves A Fall'n	page 49